Lasting Lessons

Lasting Lessons:

A Teacher's Guide to Reflecting on Experience

by
Clifford E. Knapp

Clearinghouse on Rural Education and Small Schools

ERIC

Clearinghouse on Rural Education and Small Schools
Appalachia Educational Laboratory
P.O. Box 1348
Charleston, WV 25325

Published August 1992
Printed in the United States of America
Noncommercial reproduction of portions of this document is permitted provided the ERIC Clearinghouse on Rural Education and Small Schools is credited as the source.

Second Printing August 1993
Third Printing October 1995
Fourth Printing May 1997
ISBN 1-880785-06-4

Library of Congress Cataloging-in-Publication Data

Knapp, Clifford.
    Lasting Lessons : a teacher's guide to reflecting on experi-
ence / by Clifford E. Knapp.
        p.   cm.
    Includes bibliographical references.
    ISBN 1-880785-06-4
    1. Learning, Psychology of.   2. Experiential learning.
3. Self-knowledge, Theory of.   4. Outdoor education.
I. Title.
LB1060.K62 1992
370.15'23—dc20   92-23943
                                                        CIP

    This publication was prepared with funding from the U.S. Department of Education, Office of Educational Research and Improvement, under contract no. RI-88-062016. The opinions expressed herein do not necessarily reflect the positions or policies of the Office of Educational Research and Improvement or the Department of Education.

There is a fundamental question that should be carved in stone over every school entrance to remind us all, daily, of a problem we must battle on a continual basis. That question: "Who processes the information within?" At the moment, in too many classrooms, it is teachers using texts in ignorance of the fundamental educational corollary to that question: "The extent to which the learner processes the information to be acquired is the extent to which it is acquired."

—Eliot Wigginton, Sometimes a Shining Moment: The Foxfire Experience

When a word is deprived of its dimension of action, reflection automatically suffers as well; and the word is changed into idle chatter, into verbalism, into an alienated and alienating 'blah'... On the other hand, if action is emphasized exclusively, to the detriment of reflection, the word is converted into activism. Men are not built in silence, but in word, in work, in action— reflection.

—Paulo Friere, Pedagogy of the Oppressed

The method of intelligence manifested in the experimental method demands keeping track of ideas, activities, and observed consequences. Keeping track is a matter of reflective review and summarizing, in which there is both discrimination and record of the significant features of a developing experience. To reflect is to look back over what has been done so as to extract the net meanings which are the capital stock for intelligent dealing with further experiences.

—John Dewey, Experience and Education

Students are thinking all the time, but experience teaches us that, without reflection on what we do, we are not likely to benefit from our good thinking.

—John Barell, Teaching for Thoughtfulness: Classroom Strategies to Enhance Intellectual Development

TABLE OF CONTENTS

PREFACE

This guidebook deals with the theory and practice of reflecting upon experiences. Although the discussion uses examples from outdoor education to illustrate the main ideas, teachers can apply the principles and techniques in almost any instructional setting.

An instructional activity—in fact, any activity—is potentially educational, but only when we can (a) understand its meaning and (b) apply our learning to future problems or situations. The words on the pages that follow represent, in part, my own attempt to reflect upon the sum of my experiences in order to make sense out of them and to help others make sense of theirs.

My life choices have shaped my thinking about and dispositions toward the topic of this guidebook. Especially important have been those teachers and students who have helped me learn how to reflect upon experiences more deeply and more thoroughly. My family members have helped me do this, too, especially in an emotional sense.

Jan Woodhouse has been most influential in my recent growth as a humane teacher and person. We have spent many hundreds of hours reflecting together on professional and personal activities. She, more than anyone else, has helped me make important connections between separate events, and expand the meanings and directions of my own life experiences. This guidebook is a tribute and thank you to her and the others who have helped me find my way through life's mazes and overcome the inevitable barriers, one by one.

I am grateful to Patricia Cahape and Craig Howley, staff at ERIC/CRESS, for their competent assistance in the editorial process. The reviewers of earlier drafts of the manuscript made many useful suggestions, which contributed to the quality of this final product. Also, I wish to thank Judith Young, my able typist from Northern Illinois University.

Maybe the contents of the guidebook will help teachers and other leaders clear the learning paths for their students. That's my hope and the purpose of what follows.

Clifford E. Knapp
Oregon, Illinois

CHAPTER I

Experience and Reflection: Outdoor Education and The Two Halves of Learning

Evidence is beginning to accumulate that traditional schooling's focus on individual, isolated activity, on symbols correctly manipulated but divorced from experience, and on decontextualized skills may be partly responsible for our schools' difficulty in teaching processes of thinking and knowledge construction.

—*Lauren Resnick,* Knowing, Learning, and Instruction

Typically, the goals of learning include intellectual development, personal and social development, and vocational preparation. Outdoor education—the instructional use of natural and constructed settings beyond the school to expand and enrich learning—emerged during the 1940s and 1950s as a reaction to traditional classroom-bound teaching. The teaching of that era was generally practiced as though the instructor possessed all required information and simply "poured" it into the empty heads of students.

Some educators became dissatisfied with the predominance of lectures, dependence on textbooks and other instructional technology, the fragmentation of subject-matter teaching, lack of imagination in the design of lessons, rote memorization and drill, and the excessive reliance on individual seat work. They wanted to revitalize education by moving some of it into the "real world." Outdoor education developed as one response to these circumstances.

The primary goal of outdoor educators was to establish more overall balance in the selection of both learning environments and instructional materials and methods. They saw merit in leaving the classroom occasionally to immerse students in direct experiences with people and places. They wanted fewer lessons that were mediated by symbols and traditional instructional aids. They were not convinced that one field trip per year to the zoo or fire station was adequate to achieve what they intended.

These innovators believed that students needed and wanted to learn outside in small and large groups, using more of their senses and their whole bodies as they explored meaningful problems. They wanted students to understand better the relationships between the school curriculum and community life. They realized, however, that only certain parts of the curriculum were most effectively taught and learned outside through direct experience. They were content to select only those activities judged to be most suitable to learning in settings outside the walls of the school. Additionally, these early outdoor educators knew that bringing everything inside the classroom, either directly or indirectly—for example, through various types of media—was not always appropriate.

Since the beginning, outdoor educators attempted to bring about changes in learning activities, teaching strategies, grouping arrangements, materials, and the use of instructional space. They have been less interested in changing educational goals, objectives, and the subject matter of the curriculum. Finding better ways to educate students has always been the underlying purpose of outdoor education. But, judging from a recent quote in the newsletter of the Association for Supervision and Curriculum Development (Staff, 1991, p. 6), American educators still have a long way to go:

> Mathematics and science curriculums...fail to reflect the frontiers of knowledge about how children learn best. Despite the growing influence of "constructivist" learning theory, U.S. mathematics and science curriculums sacrifice depth for coverage...fail to make connections among the disciplines, and generally ignore the real-life experiences and cognitive development of students.

In the words of Hazel Henderson (quoted in Kahn, 1978, p. 144), "Schooling is much like learning to ride a bicycle by reading about it, diagramming it on the blackboard, dissecting the bicycle—but never actually riding it."

Outdoor education is one way to improve teaching and learning through direct experience. But direct experience is not enough. If such experiences are to be meaningful and applied to life situations, teachers must help students learn from carefully planned and guided reflection sessions.

Reflection in Everyday Experiences

Reflecting upon experiences is common, and it is expected in most areas of everyday life. For instance, consider the following scenarios:

- Members of a sports team review the videotape of a recent game to identify problems in executing plays and to correct them.

- A television sports announcer interviews some players at half-time to hear their opinions of what they did well and not so well to learn what they intend to do in the second half of the game.

- A farmer examines the test plots of different corn hybrids and discusses the results with his friends before deciding what types of seed to purchase next year.

- Teachers discuss the minutes from the last faculty meeting, checking them for accuracy before voting to approve them, and then start a new meeting.

- A student teacher meets with the university supervisor to discuss a lesson just completed, with the hope of improving tomorrow's teaching.

- A driving instructor gives the student driver a few suggestions for parking closer to the curb, and the student asks for clarification before trying it again.

- The orchestra practices a difficult part of a musical piece after the conductor explains what went wrong the first time.

- A computer and television monitor are used to analyze an athlete's muscular movements, and the coach and athlete talk about how to improve future performance.

- A toothpaste manufacturer gives out free samples if the recipients agree to use them to brush their teeth before participating in a marketing survey to find out what they thought of the product.

Each of these examples entails forms of reflecting on experiences. We would rarely challenge the usefulness of the reflection inherent in these ordinary events.

But why should teachers use reflection in schools to help students enlarge (or multiply) their understandings of lessons? How could we improve teaching and learning if reflection were more frequently an essential part of instruction? When **is** it appropriate to use reflection in the learning process? Where can teachers find helpful ideas and resources to improve their ability to lead reflection sessions?

These and other questions will be explored in this guidebook, using outdoor education examples to illustrate the key points. These ideas can be used by K-12 teachers and other leaders, no matter what instructional settings they choose. So, come along and enjoy the adventure of reflecting on outdoor experiences. Don't just *do* something, *sit there* and reflect!

Cognitive Science and Implications for Outdoor Education

Why have educators been slow to incorporate reflection into the instructional routines in schools? Supposedly, it takes 25 years for innovations to be adopted in public education. Some take even longer, it seems. Perhaps we need to learn how to capture useful ideas more quickly from the world outside schools and translate them into action faster.

Recently, cognitive psychologists and information processing theorists have been gathering evidence that confirms what some of us have sensed intuitively for years about the human brain and how we learn. Educators need to apply these findings to programming, and soon. The following 12 principles represent a summary of the accumulated insights of current cognitive research and so-called "brain-based" theories of learning (see Caine & Caine, 1991, pp. 80-87). In fact, one can infer guidelines from these principles for selecting educational programs and methods. Following each principle, I have drawn some of these implications for outdoor education.

(1) **The brain is a parallel processor**
   The human brain deals with thoughts, emotions, imagination, and dispositions (attitudes toward learning) simultaneously. Outdoor education enables teachers to orchestrate experiences that address everything that the brain can process simultaneously.

(2) **Learning engages the entire physiology.**
   The three-part human brain functions according to physiological rules. Structured learning activities can inhibit or facilitate the

4

workings of the brain. Neuron growth, nourishment, and interactions relate directly to the perception and interpretation of experiences. Outdoor education involves environments that can provide relaxation, nutrition, and exercise. Some learners, in fact, get benefits that are more difficult for them to achieve in the classroom.

(3) **The search for meaning is innate.**
The search for meaning in experience and the need to act on our environment are automatic human responses. The brain naturally registers *familiar* stimuli while simultaneously searching for *novel* stimuli. Human meaning acquisition can be channelled and focused, but it cannot be stopped completely. Outdoor education provides settings that, in many cases, contain familiar as well as novel and challenging elements. Lessons conducted in the outdoors cannot only be exciting and meaningful, but frequently offer students several choices. This variety can supply most students with both familiar *and* novel stimuli to process at their present levels of readiness and in accord with past experience.

(4) **The search for meaning occurs through patterning.**
"Patterning" refers to the way the brain organizes and categorizes information. The human brain is designed to interpret and create meaning; it does not register and retain meaningless patterns over time. Outdoor education involves experiences that engage the mind in forming relevant patterns, often using activities that provide students with immediate feedback.

(5) **Emotions are critical to patterning.**
Cognitive learning never takes place in the absence of emotions or mind sets based on expectancy, personal biases, degree of self-esteem, or the need for interaction with others. Emotion, in fact, facilitates the brain's ability to store and retrieve information. Such emotions often persist long after the learning experience has ended. In the outdoors, for example, the excitement of finding a snake, the fear of the night, and the peace that accompanies a sunset can color the depth of cognitive learning and become significant and lasting memories.

(6) **The brain processes parts and wholes simultaneously.**
The human brain is divided into left and right hemispheres. In healthy people, the two hemispheres interact in the process of learning. One part reduces information into parts and the other perceives it as a whole, or series of wholes. Outdoor education,

when conducted skillfully, provides a natural setting for viewing parts in context among wholes.

(7) **Learning involves both focused attention and peripheral perception.**
The human brain absorbs information both within the focus of awareness and from outside it. Peripheral stimuli can influence the lesson because the brain responds to the entire sensory context in which the lesson occurs. Outdoor education provides a rich source of peripheral stimuli (including people) to engage learning. Teachers who are genuinely comfortable outdoors project this awareness, enhancing the importance of the lesson to students.

(8) **Learning always involves conscious and unconscious processes.**
Human beings absorb information both consciously and unconsciously, at the same time. For this reason, we remember total learning experiences, not just the "telling" that usually constitutes instruction. Outdoor education often incorporates experiential learning methods, and reflection is important to experiential learning. Reflection helps students become more aware of how and what they learn, and it entails both conscious and unconscious processes.

(9) **We have at least two different types of memory: A spatial memory system and a set of systems for rote learning.**
The brain has two primary memory systems. The first is the spatial system, which needs no rehearsal and allows for "instant" memory of experiences. It is designed for registering experience in three-dimensional space, and the human capacity for such memory increases with time. The second is the system for rote learning. This system deals with isolated facts and skills; the brain needs more practice and rehearsal in order to retain them. The more separated this kind of information is from prior knowledge and actual experience, however, the greater the need for practice and rehearsal. Outdoor education usually capitalizes on the personal worlds of learners by engaging the "instant" memory systems through direct experience.

(10) **We understand and remember best when facts and skills are embedded in natural, spatial memory.**
What we learn is shaped by our internal processes and our social environment. All education can be enhanced when specific

information is part of the context of meaningful experience. Outdoor education teaches "in context." It deals with specific facts, concepts, skills, attitudes, and values in the context of

Geology learned first hand is geology fused in the mind forever. (Photograph by George Tarbay, Art-Photo Dept., Northern Illinois University)

firsthand experience. This tendency reduces the need for the extended rehearsal and practice that rote memory working alone requires.

(11) **Learning is enhanced by challenge and inhibited by threat.**
When students perceive threat their brains "downshift." Students who sense serious threat become mentally rigid. In this state they often revert to automatic, and even primitive, routines of behavior. Outdoor education, however, provides supportive learning climates and challenging lessons, with a base in students' interests.

(12) **Each brain is unique.**
Everyone's memory systems are integrated differently, and because learning changes the structure of the brain, individuals become even *more unique* as they grow and learn. Outdoor education works in a setting that cultivates this individuality. Students can express a much wider range of visual, tactile, emotional, and auditory preferences than is possible in a classroom. That is, students have greater freedom to develop the disposition to learn.

These 12 principles suggest that educators—both those who teach in the outdoors and those who teach (as yet) only in classrooms—need to provide for reflection in their instruction and in their curriculum. We need not wait 25 years in order to begin to expand the meanings of experiences in the minds of our students.

Six Illustrative Scenarios
Described next are several scenarios that illustrate how we might do this.

Scenario #1. A sixth-grade class learned about dichotomous keys for identifying trees before going out on the school grounds to use them. After Mrs. Jones guided the class in keying out a maple tree together, the students divided into trios and were asked to find a different tree to identify it cooperatively. After a while, she gathered the students in a circle for a discussion and asked some questions to help sharpen their skills, pausing after each question to give students time to formulate their responses:

- How many think you used the key correctly to identify your tree?
- How could you be sure you were right?

The sense of wonder is re-awakened in students as they discover a nest.
(Photograph by Northern Illinois University Art/Photo, DeKalb, IL)

- Did you ever get "off track" and then correct yourself?

- Did any of you discover a helpful tip in using the key that you will share with the whole group?

Then the teacher asked her students to find another tree or continue where they had left off, applying what they had just learned from the reflection session.

Scenario #2. The seventh-grade class had been studying figures of speech in language arts. After a practice session in the classroom, Mr. Smith paired the students and asked them to go to the park two blocks away and write a short poem together, using at least five different figures of speech. After about twenty minutes, he gathered the students and asked each pair to read one example from their poem. Then the teacher asked for volunteers to give suggestions for working together more productively. After listening awhile, the students created a metaphor—using what they learned from writing poetry together—to apply to future cooperative projects.

Scenario #3. Students in a tenth-grade class decided to write their own mathematics book using measurement problems to be solved outside. To illustrate one type of problem, Ms. Phillips divided the class into groups and provided a handout describing four different ways to calculate the height of trees. She supplied the necessary equipment, and the groups went out to try the methods

After noticing that some groups were struggling with the assignment, the teacher called the class together. She asked them to imagine that someone had just videotaped them solving the problems. After giving them time to imagine what this videotape would look like, the teacher asked for volunteers to narrate their imaginary tapes—in as much detail as possible. Whenever a student mentioned something that applied to the difficulties observed, she stopped the speaker and emphasized the points. After listening to several "tape" narrations, the students went back to their tasks.

Scenario #4. A fourth-grade teacher, Mr. Black, observed that some class members were not listening very well to each other and were running into trouble working as a team. He recalled an activity in which students had paired up to gather matching numbers and sizes of sticks, stones, acorns, and other natural objects. He then seated the students back to back in pairs, and one in each pair chose to be the "leader" and the other the "follower." This exercise then took place:

Each leader placed the objects, one at a time, on the ground in a certain pattern. When the design was completed, the leader then explained how to place the items so the follower could reconstruct the

Walking together on the boards can teach teamwork through experience.
(Photograph by Tom Lesser)

same pattern without seeing it. The followers remained silent.

After a while, the teacher spoke so that every student pair could hear him. He asked:

- Did the leaders purposely make a simple pattern or a complex one?

- As the follower, what were you thinking as you arranged the objects?

- As the leader, do you think your directions were clear? Does your partner agree with you?

- How could the follower become a better listener?

- As you continue this exercise, how could you improve your skills as a listener and direction giver?

After giving the students more time to continue where they left off, he asked his students to stop once again and draw a diagram showing how each person saw the pair working. After comparing the diagrams, the teacher asked the students to volunteer statements about the importance of these skills to an upcoming class project.

Scenario #5. A ninth-grade social studies class was involved in a unit about the local early settlers. To help the students get a better feeling for everyday life before modern technology, Mr. Redd prepared a list of tasks that pioneers might do with the simple tools available at the time. These tasks were:

(1) cook apple butter,

(2) dip candles,

(3) build a fire,

(4) make brooms, and

(5) build wooden toys.

After the work teams were formed and the projects chosen, the class went to a nearby "pioneer village," where they could practice their skills. As the teacher roamed from group to group, he observed that

Learning how to saw a log can be a long-time memory and a way to appreciate pioneer life. (Photograph by George Tarbay, Art-Photo Dept., Northern Illinois University)

the boys in most groups were giving orders to the girls and in most instances were taking more active roles. At lunch time, therefore, he started a discussion by sharing this observation. After a while, he invited the students to think about the roles of males and females and to write one question to ask that would help them understand the situation better.

Back at school, these questions were discussed, one by one, to broaden the students' perspectives about gender issues. What had begun as a lesson on pioneer life, ended as a session on modern-day sex-role stereotypes.

Scenario #6.   A third-grade teacher decided to expand the students' awareness of color found outside on the school grounds. First, Ms. Toms read the poem, "What is Green?" in *Hailstones and Halibut Bones*, by Mary O'Neill (New York: Doubleday and Company, 1961). Then she gave the students a piece of light-colored sandpaper and told them to find as many shades of green as possible and rub a small color blotch on the sandpaper. Before starting, the students were asked to predict how many different shades they would find and write that number on the back of their sandpaper. Then the teacher raised questions about what plants should not be picked and why. After the students agreed on some picking rules, they spread out to find as many shades of green as possible within ten minutes. When time was up, the teacher gathered the students and put them in groups of four. She asked them to discuss the following questions, one at a time:

- Were you surprised about anything you found?

- Which is your favorite shade of green? Where did it come from?

- If you were to create a picture titled, "A Study in Green," what would it look like?

- Were you right about your prediction?

- What green-colored objects did you find for the first time on the school grounds?

- If you were asked to find shades of brown and rub them on sandpaper, where would you look?

Then Ms. Toms gave them another piece of sandpaper, asked them to write down their predictions of how many browns they'd find, and to begin the new assignment.

Discussing the colors found in nature. (Photograph by George Tarbay, Art-Photo Dept., Northern Illinois University)

Summarizing the Scenarios

Let's review each scenario to discover some common threads. In #1 Mrs. Jones asked several questions directed at improving student skills in using tree keys. Based on what they learned, they then continued the activity.

In #2 the students shared an example of how they used one figure of speech in their poem and offered tips on what they had learned about working with a partner. Using this information, they continued writing.

In #3 the students were asked to make an imaginary videotape of their math activity and narrate it for others. Ms. Phillips underscored the relevant points and then asked the students to continue.

In #4 Mr. Black structured an interpersonal skill activity on listening and giving directions. After asking them to consider some well-directed questions, the students continued the activity. Later, he asked them to draw a diagram that showed how they perceived the pairs working together. After comparing these diagrams, the students drew conclusions to be applied to an upcoming class project.

In #5 Mr. Redd had first intended to have his students become more sensitive to pioneer living, but as the lesson developed, he noticed the males taking dominant roles. Taking a new direction, he asked the students to create questions that might help them improve awareness of sex-role stereotyping in their class.

In #6 Ms. Toms structured small group discussions focused on discovering shades of green. Then the students planned a strategy for finding shades of brown before going out to complete the new task.

In each case, the teacher actively intervened at certain points during the outdoor activity in order to structure a session *designed to help students reflect upon what had happened*. Through the use of different reflection strategies, the teachers helped students make connections between actions and consequences, but also to raise their awareness of objects and events so that they could apply what they learned in future situations.

Common to all these scenarios, then, is the intentional use of a reflection phase in the teaching/learning cycle. The purpose of this guidebook is to explore this feature of educational practice in greater depth. It should be clearer to you now, why such a consideration is so important. Caine and Caine (1991, p. 147) put it well:

> To maximize connections, gain deeper insights, and perceive the additional possibilities that are hidden in experience, we have to deliberately and consciously work for them. This work is roughly like processing the ore from mining to extract the maximum value. Students usually lack both the skill and the necessary awareness to search for deeper implications.

A Rose By Any Other Name

Gertrude Stein once said, "A rose is a rose is a rose." By whatever name we call the common feature of the six preceding scenarios, we are still describing the same thing. The idea of reflection has carried many synonyms in the educational literature. Some of these other words are: debriefing, processing, active processing, critiquing, closure, elaboration, bridging, reviewing, thinking about thinking (metacognition), critical thinking, facilitating, analyzing, publishing, generalizing, teaching for transfer, evaluating, interviewing, inquiry, design, and consideration. Perhaps the most frequently used synonyms for what I mean by reflection, however, are "debriefing" and "processing." These synonyms will be most familiar to outdoor educators.

The chosen term for this guidebook, "reflect," comes from the Latin, "reflectere," meaning "to bend back." Just as a mirror bends back light rays to the observer's eye, so reflection bends back (to the mind's eye) features of an experience that might otherwise have gone unseen.

Examining Definitions of Reflection and Related Terms

Let's pause now to examine some different definitions of reflection and related terms (that is, let's reflect on the meaning of the key word for this guidebook!).

- Debriefing occurs when participants in a learning activity, ... are led through a session in which they relive parts of their experience in a supportive environment and draw conclusions from it.
  (Boud, Keogh, & Walker, 1985, p. 16)

- Reflection is an important human activity in which people recapture their experience, think about it, mull it over, and evaluate it.
  (Boud et al., 1985, p. 19)

- Reflection in the context of learning is a generic term for those intellectual and affective activities [that] lead to new understandings and appreciations.
  (Boud et al., 1985, p. 19)

- In 1916, Dewey defined reflection as "...a process which perceives connections and links between the parts of an experience.
  (Boud et al., 1985, p. 25)

- Debriefing is that phase in experience-based learning where purposeful reflection by an individual or group takes place.
  (Pearson & Smith, 1985, p. 70)

- Reflection is a process of transformation of the determinate "raw material" of our experiences...into determinate products (understandings, commitments, actions), a transformation effected by our determinate labour (our thinking about the relationship between thought and action, and the relationship between the individual and society), using determinate means of production (communication, decision-making, and action).
  (Kemmis, 1985, p. 148)

- [Reviewing is] the process of analyzing personal/group experience in order to learn from it more effectively.
  (Hunt & Hitchin, 1989, p. 74)

- Processing is an activity which is employed for the purpose of encouraging the learner to reflect, describe, analyze, and communicate in some way that that which was recently experienced.
  (Quinsland & Van Ginkel, 1984, p. 9)

16

- The concept of reflectivity is a reasoned, principled response through either pre-planned or spontaneous but conscious action in which awareness of past experience and understandings are linked with present experience to lead to new understandings and appreciations.

  (Fellows & Zimpher, 1988, p. 19)

- Active processing...is the consolidation and internalization of information, by the learner, in a way that is both personally meaningful and conceptually coherent.

  (Caine & Caine, 1991, p. 147)

Each of these definitions describes the same phase of the learning process, though each emphasizes different concepts. The word "experience," however, appears in all but the last. It seems that experience is the basis of reflection.

In reflection, the learner is either becoming aware, transforming, analyzing, recapturing, reliving, exploring, or linking the parts of an experience. The goals, products, or ends of reflection are: new understandings or appreciations; commitments; the learning of meaningful and conceptually coherent information; or action. The means to achieve these ends are either drawing conclusions, communicating, evaluating, decisionmaking, thinking about relationships, or describing, often (in the case of learning activities) within a supportive group environment. General agreement about the nature of reflection clearly exists, though authors emphasize different concepts to explain it.

The aim of reflection, simply put, is to promote meaningful experience. According to Csikszentmihalyi (1990, pp. 216-217), "Creating meaning involves bringing order to the contents of the mind by integrating one's actions into a unified flow experience." Achieving meaning involves:

(1)   a goal that can give significance to life,

(2)   which is translated into action, and

(3)   results in a recognition of harmony among feelings, thoughts, and actions.

This three-part definition of "meaning" is useful in guiding reflection during experiential learning.

17

Several authors note the vital need for reflection. They claim that this phase of learning is often overlooked, purposely ignored, or poorly conducted. Typical of the concerns expressed about the problem of not using reflection time or not doing it well are the following quotes:

- Unfortunately, it is infrequently used in schools. In our informal survey of schools we visited, even the outstanding ones tended to leave reflection largely to chance or the counselor's office.
  (Caine & Caine, 1991, p. 149)

- It [reflection] is...the activity we are least accustomed to doing, and therefore the activity we will have to be the most rigorous in including, and for which we will have to help students develop skills.
  (Staff, 1990, p. 2)

- The skill of experiential learning in which people tend to be the most deficient is reflection.
  (Duley, 1981, p. 611)

- I can very often strongly sense in some people a great resistance to any form of reflection on their educational experience.
  (Main, 1985, p. 98)

- Sharing one's reactions is only the first step. An essential—and often neglected—part of the cycle is the necessary integration of this sharing. The dynamics that emerged in the activity are explored, discussed, and evaluated (processed) with other participants.
  (Jones & Pfeiffer, 1979, pp. 189-190)

In the next section, we will examine some key terms: knowledge and knowing, thinking, experience, learning, and transfer. This vocabulary will be useful to us in describing some ways of reflecting. The concepts can also help teachers justify leading reflection sessions.

What Is Knowledge And Knowing?

To know the world, one must construct it.
—*Cesare Pavese*

What is knowledge? What does it mean to know something? Most people agree that the main purpose of an education is to increase a

18

learner's knowledge. However, we sometimes act in error if we assume that others really understand what we mean by "knowledge."

When I "know" the name of a bird such as a chickadee, I can identify it by sight or sound. Thus, when I see a small black, white, and gray bird with a cap-like marking on its head, the experience triggers something in my brain, and I say, "chickadee." When I hear certain sounds—even if I don't actually see the bird—I also "know" it is chickadee.

Naming the bird from visual or aural clues may, however, be all I know about chickadees! Obviously, there is much more to learn about its behavior, ecology, and interactions with humans. Naming something is a shallow form of knowing, but it can be an important beginning for building my knowledge category (or "schema") about birds and chickadees.

Another way to "know" something is to demonstrate a specific skill such as fire-building. I "know" how to take matches or flint and steel, along with combustible materials, and make a fire. I may not be able to write, or describe how I do this, but I can prove I "know" by demonstrating my capacity to build a real fire.

Traditionally, schools have honored the first way of knowing (chickadee-naming) more than the second way (fire-building). Educators have also honored identifying pictures of chickadees more than labeling the real bird in the field. More often, they have assessed student knowledge by the answers students supply on paper, rather than by the accuracy of their field identification or by their performances.

Gardner (1985, pp. 68) describes these two ways of knowing as "know-that" (propositional knowledge about the actual set of procedures involved in execution) and "know-how" (tacit knowledge of how to execute something). Plato made the same distinction over two thousand years ago.

Marzano and colleagues (1988, pp. 13-14) labeled the "know-that" way as declarative knowledge and the action-based, "know-how" way as procedural knowledge. To these two types of knowledge, they added a third, called conditional knowledge. This type refers to knowing *why* a given strategy works or *when* to use one strategy rather than another. This third kind of knowing is important because, without it, declarative and procedural knowledge cannot be used properly in the real world.

Caine and Caine (1991, p. 101) describe "natural knowledge"—all categories and other structures that organize our perception. We can usually access these categories almost instantly (birds, trees, rocks) without having to think about them consciously.

In other words, when I see that small, black-capped bird, I don't have to think very hard before the word "chickadee" comes to mind. Other observers of the same bird might register only, "bird," when they see the chickadee. They might have to wrack their brains to remember its special name. Easily accessed information such as that necessary to identify the chickadee is surface knowledge—content devoid of significance to the learner (Caine & Caine, 1991, p. 93).

Whitehead referred to this sort of knowledge as "inert"—ideas that students cannot relate to evident applications (1929, p. 17). William Glasser (1992, p. 691) labeled this knowledge "throwaway information" or "nonsense"—learned only to pass tests and not used at all later on. To many people, "knowing" the information needed to identify a chickadee is unimportant—precisely because it lacks meaning. Perhaps to them "knowing" that the small animal is a bird is enough, if they notice or care about it at all. Surface knowledge is something a robot can be programmed to know. We can memorize surface knowledge, but without understanding and use, we soon forget it.

Unfortunately, much of what we have called education in schools has consisted of surface knowledge. After a written test, the usefulness of surface knowledge disappears, and usually it is soon forgotten. The point to remember for teaching, however, is simple:

> Both natural knowledge (accessible categories and classifications that organize experience) and surface knowledge (bits of information devoid of meaning) can work together.

Memorizing certain things, such as the word, "chickadee," can, for example, take place in the context of an exciting experience at a bird-banding station. In this way, the students' natural knowledge of birds, applied to the capture of a particular bird in a mist net, can serve as a way of remembering the name of the bird and its habits.

According to Resnick (1989, p. 3), knowledge is retained only when (1) embedded in organizing structures and (2) closely connected to the situation in which learning takes place. The outdoors supplies abundant sources on which natural knowledge can work, and teachers can use those sources to construct activities that create interesting memories that stay with students for many years. The outdoors is a good context—though by no means the only context—to act on Resnick's insight.

Resnick and Klopfer (1989, p. 5) also describe another kind of knowledge, used to interpret new situations, solve problems, and to think and reason. This they call "generative" knowledge. Generative knowledge is prior knowledge that can produce (or "generate") *new* knowledge.

In order to accumulate generative knowledge, however, students must elaborate upon and question their experiences. They must examine new information in relation to previously held information, and expand their existing knowledge structures. One way for doing this could be a planned, teacher-led reflection session.

Figure 1 illustrates these types of knowledge and suggests relationships among them. One might show these relationships in other ways, of course, but Figure 1 illustrates several points relevant to the topic of this guidebook. First, surface knowledge is a kind of declarative

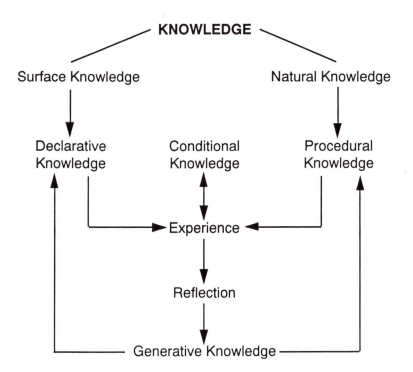

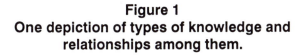

Figure 1
One depiction of types of knowledge and relationships among them.

21

knowledge separated from experience and reflection. It contributes little to further learning (one reason it is so soon forgotten). Second, in many classrooms, links between declarative knowledge and experience are weak. Finally, Figure 1 illustrates a cycle of knowledge. In this cycle, all types of knowledge (except surface knowledge) can help students generate new knowledge through experience and reflection.

These examples suggest that there are different types of knowledge and degrees of knowing. At the same time, however, we need to realize that the kinds of things we know also vary. Gardner (1985, p. 70) describes six categories of knowledge (which he labels "intelligences"—abilities to solve problems or create valued products):

- linguistic,

- musical,

- logical-mathematical,

- spatial,

- bodily-kinesthetic, and

- personal (intrapersonal and interpersonal).

Knowing about knowing can help teachers formulate the kinds of questions and structured activities necessary for conducting reflection sessions. Pearson and Smith (1988, p. 75) notes that "different types of knowledge suggest different forms and approaches to the debriefing process, and different relationships between participants and the group leader."

What Is Thinking?

Thinking is more interesting than knowing, but less interesting than looking.
—Johann Wolfgang von Goethe

For Beyer (1987), thinking is the process of making sense of experience—an individual's search for *meaning*. Thinking involves an array of complex mental skills, applied to gain understanding. Beyer describes this process as follows:

Thinking is a holistic process by which we mentally manipulate sensory input and recalled data to formulate thoughts, reason about, or judge. It involves perception, prior experience, conscious manipulation, incubation, and intuition. (1987, p. 37)

Definitions vary, but educators generally agree on some of the important features of thinking. According to Resnick (1987, p. 46) thinking is composed of:

(1) generating multiple ideas,

(2) recognizing alternative viewpoints on a topic,

(3) summarizing what has been experienced,

(4) figuring out meanings from events,

(5) solving problems, and

(6) identifying fallacies and false conclusions.

Marzano and colleagues (1988, pp. 146-148) have constructed a framework with four "dimensions" of thinking, as follows:

(1) **Metacognition** (awareness and control of one's own thinking, including commitment, attitudes, and attention),

(2) **Critical Thinking** (deciding what to believe or do) and creative thinking (forming new combinations of ideas to meet a need),

(3) **Thinking Processes** (complex sequences of skills to either form concepts, principles, new meanings, and problem solutions; or to conduct scientific inquiry, develop new products, or talk with people), and

(4) **Core Thinking Skills** (building blocks of thinking; for example, focusing, information gathering, remembering, organizing, analyzing, producing new information or ideas, combining information, or evaluating).

In 1982, the Education Commission of the States listed the following major thinking operations: evaluation, analysis, critical thinking, problem solving, synthesis, and decisionmaking (cited in Beyer, 1987, pp. 1-2).

If one of the aims of a reflection session is to help students think, then teachers need to keep the key features of thinking in view. These features are useful in planning questions and structuring activities for reflecting on experience.

What Is Experience?

The Latin word, "experientia," meaning "to go through," is one source of our word "experience." The Middle English and French source for the word means "experiment." One might therefore claim that the modern word means "to go through an experiment." This claim rests on the fact that, in one sense, all of our interactions with the environment are experiments. We can never completely know—or accurately predict—the outcomes of our actions.

What we gain from these "experiments" depends upon our understanding of as many of the factors involved as possible. According to Sarason (1984, pp. 224-225), "You do not learn by doing...you learn by thinking-acting-thinking-acting...In and of itself, doing, like experiencing, can be a mindless affair."

Reflection can be used to analyze our experiments with life to find the patterns that connect them. Dewey, Whitehead, Montessori, and others believed that much of what we learn is gathered from firsthand experience, but, according to Caine and Caine (1991), we continue to ignore the hidden depth of the phrase, "learn from experience." Reflection is a good way to open this hidden depth to students.

Caine and Caine (1991, p. 104) use a broad definition of the word, "experience." They contend that life immerses us in some type of experience at every moment of our lives, much as water surrounds a fish. In short, these authors believe that *all* learning is experiential. The key to successful learning, then, depends on the wise use of experience, including the selection of experiences that are appropriate for and meaningful to learners.

According to Caine and Caine (1991, p. 85), cognitive research suggests that human beings possess "a natural, spatial memory system that does not need rehearsal and allows for 'instant' memory of experiences....[This] system is always engaged and is inexhaustible." This type of memory is used best through interactive, real-life activity such as projects, field trips, visual imagery, stories, drama, and metaphor exercises. Even more significantly, cognitive science confirms that people are creatures who make meaning. Their search for meaning cannot be stopped, only channelled and focused.

Many educators today have come to believe that students construct their own knowledge from experience, rather than believing that teachers impose knowledge on students as a complete package. Caine and Caine (1991, pp. 104-105) offer guidance to teachers who take this view. According to them, good instruction requires that:

(1) teachers orchestrate the immersion of the learner in complex, interactive experiences;

(2) experiences be viewed by the learner as personally meaningful challenges; and

(3) learners gain insight about a problem through intensive analysis ("active processing").

The purpose of a reflection session is to channel and focus the meanings that students inevitably try to derive from experiences. Reflection sessions, then, mediate experience in order to help students make meaning.

Schooling, in general, also mediates experiences. Words, numbers, and pictures; lectures, books and other writing; computers, posters, films, slides, and videos—all the "media" of instruction—stand between students and immediate experience. And, in fact, reflection requires distance. At the same time, reflection—as we have seen— requires experience. One reason inert or surface knowledge is so common in schools, however, may be that students encounter too little meaningful experience. That is, instruction seldom involves the direct experience and reflection that learning requires.

What Is Learning?

Learning is the process of acquiring and constructing knowledge. It depends upon elaborating and extending prior knowledge. When students want to learn a particular thing, they engage in "intentional" learning. We can say we have acquired learning in this sense, for example, when we can recover a body of information some time after acquiring it by the senses—perhaps to apply what we learned in a new situation.

Cognitive scientists have also formulated a new instructional theory, based on the assumption that students construct knowledge from guided experiences. According to Resnick and Klopfer (1989, p. 4), "Thinking and learning merge in today's cognitive perspective." Wigginton reflects this view in practical terms:

Learning which leads to the retention, use, and articulation of knowledge happens when we progress from meaningful experience *to* texts and/or teachers...to evaluation and analysis and reflection, and then back to 'hands-on' experience again.

(Wigginton, 1986, p. 208)

25

The teacher is still a key person in the learning process, especially during the reflection phase. Reflection without the guiding light of goals and objectives can only be aimless and unproductive—for all concerned.

What Is Transfer?

After we teach a lesson on tree identification and wood properties outdoors, will the students know how to buy the best kind of lumber to build a bird house? Not necessarily. There is no guarantee that a student can transfer something learned in one setting to another setting. The process of applying knowledge learned in one setting to another situation is called "transfer." According to Perkins and Salomon (1988, p. 23),

> The implicit assumption in educational practice has been that transfer takes care of itself. To be lighthearted about a heavy problem, one might call this the 'Bo Peep' theory of transfer: 'Let them alone and they'll come home wagging their tails behind them.'

Current research on transfer, however, does not provide clear answers to questions dealing with the transferability of knowledge to different settings. Research on transfer has not fully explored the effects of instruction that combines practice in thinking skills with meaningful subject matter content—only the effects of one or the other alone. Resnick (1987, p. 19) notes that "the view that we can expect strong transfer from learning in one area to improvements across the board has never been well supported empirically." The open questions are: Why? How? and Under what circumstances?

Though research has not yet answered such questions, teachers will continue to expect that what they teach will transfer later in some ways. Moreover, learning transfer evidently *does* take place. For example, it seems reasonable, at least intuitively, that some lessons learned outdoors will transfer to similar outdoor situations. If, on a trip to the woods, we actually show students how to find their way out of a forest by following natural water courses, we trust that they will be likely to use that information when actually lost. We may also believe that such transfer will be more likely than if they had only been told or read about this survival skill in the classroom.

Perkins and Salomon (1988, p. 25) describe two mechanisms of transfer—"low-road" transfer and "high-road" transfer. Low-road transfer is illustrated by the ability to drive a truck after being taught in a car. Most trucks are similar enough to a car so that a person can usually apply the knowledge originally learned in the car. This type of transfer involves the automatic triggering of well-practiced routines from one setting to another similar one.

High-road transfer, on the other hand, depends more on deliberate abstraction of knowledge from one context to another. In this case, the learning environment does not closely resemble the application setting. For example, if students are successful in listening, giving directions, and giving and taking feedback in order to get their entire group to balance on a stump, they may be able to transfer these interpersonal skills to cooperatively writing a book back at school—providing, of course, that they have the necessary writing skills. The degree to which the students are able to make the connections between what was learned on the stump that might apply to working together on another project, determines the usefulness and amount of transfer from one experience to another.

Viewing transfer as either low-road or high-road can be helpful in structuring the reflection session with students. Anticipated high-road transfer situations may require more specific questions and techniques to help students link the outdoor experience to contextually different future applications. If the teacher aims for high-road transfer, but fails to cultivate the necessary connections, whatever is learned about teamwork on the stump could easily become inert or surface knowledge.

Gass (1990, pp. 200-201) describes three transfer theories. The first two, specific and nonspecific transfer, are similar to low- and high-road transfer. However, Gass' specific transfer is limited mostly to skills. Nonspecific transfer, by contrast, usually applies to principles and attitudes. In other words, attitudes about teamwork learned in the stump activity could be explicitly taught for subsequent application, for example, to the situation of writing a book together.

Gass (1990, p. 201) also describes a third kind of transfer, called "metaphoric transfer." This sort of transfer requires students to generalize principles from one learning situation to another in the form of an analogy or metaphor. The given example of this theory describes a person who has learned how to paddle a canoe with others and realizes that the canoe moves forward smoothly when everyone uses the paddles correctly. When they don't, the canoe veers from side to side, and their progress is "jerky."

The canoe metaphor could be applied to how a group works together on a different task, and such an application may influence the outcome. In a reflection session, the teacher might help the students identify analogies and metaphors that could apply to future situations. The teacher could ask, "how is figuring out how to unravel a human knot like cooperatively writing a school play?"

Bracey (1992) summarized findings about the transfer of learning in a recent article. According to him, studies of transfer suggest that learning is centered in particular contexts. The difficulty lies in determining how and when transfer takes place, and, given such knowledge, devising teaching that improves transfer. Bracey (p. 728) concludes that transfer from one context to another is unlikely unless people are "somehow alerted to the fact that the two contexts can be seen as similar." Teacher-led reflection sessions may be one way to increase the likelihood of transfer, especially if teachers make clear to students the future contexts to which the learning applies.

When Did Reflection Begin: How Has It Evolved?

Is reflective inquiry simply new wine in old wineskins?
(Houston, 1988, p. 7)

According to Houston (1988, pp. 7-8), the concept of reflection is ancient. The wisdom of elders and prophets was based on their ability to analyze situations and problems, to think divergently, and propose solutions to problems. In Greece, Plato and Aristotle; in China, Confucius and Lao Tzu; in the Middle East, Solomon; and in India, Gautama the Buddha exhibited the skills and habits of reflection. Centuries later, of course, the great European philosophers used reflection in their work—constructing modern science in the process. Later still, Whitehead and Dewey developed reflection as an approach to teaching.

The earliest use of the term revolved around individual thinkers applying the idea of reflection to themselves and their own circumstances in the world. Comparatively few examples survive of how these wise people may have helped others learn through the process of reflection (except through surviving printed works).

One striking exception to this observation is Socrates. Socrates, noted Greek teacher and thinker, spent much of his life trying to discover the nature of goodness by asking questions of others. He encouraged the Athenian citizens to search for knowledge, act on it, and

28

to live life in association with others in accord with their knowledge. He constantly challenged the statements and beliefs of the people around him, including Plato, one of his students.

His approach was to probe a topic with others until he discovered the essential truths about it. This way of relating to others became known as the "dialectic," "inquiry," or "Socratic" method. Frost (1942, p. 236) summarizes the Socratic method:

> It consists of taking a statement made by another and so analyzing it as to reveal its inconsistencies. Then, after the other person recognizes the fallacies in his view, the questioner asks him a series of questions in which he brings out what he believes to be the truth. (Frost, 1942, p. 236)

Since questioning is used to a great extent in the process of reflection, more details of Socratic questioning will be dealt with in Chapter III.

Dewey's contributions. John Dewey (1916) explained his views on experience and thinking in his book, *Democracy and Education*. He believed that experience included both active and passive elements. He explained, "When we experience something we act upon it, we do something with it; then we suffer or undergo the consequences" (1916, p. 163). Dewey thought that the degree to which we connect actions and consequences constitutes a measure of the value of the experience.

Experience, with Dewey, had to be more than "mere activity" without thought. His aim was to use experiences to change individuals by helping them reflect and become consciously aware of how actions are connected to the resulting consequences. He illustrated this idea with the example of sticking a finger into a flame. The act becomes an experience only when it is connected with the resulting pain. From that point on in life, sticking your finger in a flame *means* a burn because you clearly link the act with the consequences.

Dewey wanted education to consist of meaningful experiences so that students could better predict future results, consequently gaining more control over their own lives. He wanted students "to make a backward and forward connection between what we do to things and what we enjoy or suffer from things in consequence" (1916, p. 164). He encouraged students to learn by linking their minds directly with physical activities. He pointed out three "evil results" from separating the mind and body:

(1) Using the body could become a distraction to contend with in schools because it is viewed as not being useful to achieve significant results. The body would then become something to keep still so the mind could go about the serious business of learning.

(2) When the senses and certain muscles are merely used to take in what is in a book, on a map or blackboard, or to write something, without seeing a purpose for it or recognizing its meaning (beyond pleasing the teacher or earning a grade), it becomes a mechanical act and not an intellectual one.

(3) Separating the mind from direct occupation with things takes the emphasis away from understanding the relationships among them.

In reality, every perception involves judgment and seeing things in relationships. Dewey illustrated this point by explaining how we understand the meaning of the term, "chair." We fully know the concept, "chair," only by connecting it to something else—its purpose, place in time or space, or other relationship—not by its isolated qualities such as height, weight, or size of parts.

Words are shallow substitutes for ideas—unless their connections to ideas are based in vital experiences requiring judgments that link the words (and the ideas!) together. For Dewey, relationships could be perceived only through experience. He believed that, lacking experiences, we would possess half-observations. He wrote, "An ounce of experience is better than a ton of theory simply because it is only in experience that any theory has vital and verifiable significance" (1916, p. 169).

Dewey viewed the terms "thought" and "reflection" as synonymous. He defined them both as "the discernment of the relation between what we try to do and what happens in consequence" (1916, p. 169). He contrasted two types of experience, each defined according to the proportion of reflection involved.

In one case, trial and error experience involves doing something and when it fails, doing something else, until we hit upon something that works. Then we use that approach to solve subsequent problems that are similar. When we fail to fully understand the connections between our actions and the resulting consequences, we may or may not solve a problem using this approach.

The other type, reflective experience, involves analyzing how the cause and effect are related. If we know more about this relationship, we can then better predict results by knowing how the different variables affect the outcome of our actions. The more we are aware of the conditions of a situation, the better we can predict or control the outcomes.

Reflection, then, in Dewey's view "is the intentional endeavor to discover *specific* connections between something which we do and the consequence which results, so that the two come continuous" (1916, p. 170). We can then understand why things happen as they do. Of course, in this view of reflection, having aims is a necessary condition of inferring the results of future actions. In the Deweyan view, reflection, then, involves accepting responsibility for future consequences that flow from a chosen action. Accordingly, "To consider the *bearing* of the occurrence upon what may be, but is not yet, is to think" (Dewey, 1916, p. 172). Reflection involves a personal concern with the issue. We must identify with the outcomes of a course of events in order to think about them. For Dewey, thinking and reflecting thus possess distinctly ethical qualities. People's responsibility rests on their ability to reflect on the consequences of their actions—social as well as personal consequences. Responsibility, of course, is important precisely because all action (and the reflection necessary to understand action) involves a risk and an adventure into the unknown.

In summary, Dewey described a reflective experience as involving:

(1) a certain amount of confusion and doubt because the situation is incomplete;

(2) a tentative interpretation of the given elements and how they will lead to certain consequences;

(3) a careful survey of the elements, which defines and clarifies the problem;

(4) an elaboration of the tentative hypothesis to make it more precise; and

(5) the taking of an action that tests the hypothesis.

The extent and accuracy of steps 3 and 4 distinguish a reflective experience from a trial and error experience. Dewey cautioned us to realize that we can never completely go beyond trial and error experience. We always need to try out our plan in the real world before we know if it will work. Since we can never know all the connections between actions and consequences, we cannot make accurate predictions all of the time.

Piaget's contributions. Jean Piaget, more than 50 years ago, argued that people are builders of knowledge structures and not simply passive recorders of information. He believed that knowledge acquired by memorizing alone was neither real nor useful knowledge. Piagetian theory stressed the need for understanding through constructive activities undertaken when the learner was at the appropriate stage of readiness. Modern cognitive theory has come to honor Piaget's beliefs in this area, as well as to recognize the important roles of prior knowledge and guided instruction in making meaning.

Piaget believed that people constantly attempt to make sense of the world in which they live. Gardner, reflecting the Piagetian view, described this process as follows:

> The individual is continually constructing hypotheses and thereby attempting to generate knowledge: He is trying to figure out the nature of material objects in the world, how they interact with one another, as well as the nature of persons in the world, their motivations and their behavior.
>
> (Gardner, 1985, p. 18)

Piaget's theory of thought structures describes how abstract thought develops from concrete experience. Meyers (1987, p. 27) describes abstract thinking as "the ability to identify principles or concepts in specific experiences that can be generalized to other experiences."

According to Piagetian theory, children pass through stages of intellectual development as they mature. For example, between the ages of six and eleven, children begin to generalize and categorize information (for example, kinds of birds). Piaget labeled this stage "concrete-operational" because of the necessary link to the concrete (tangible) world and the mental operation of logical reasoning. Piaget's fourth stage—formal-operational—is supposed to occur between the ages of eleven and sixteen and should enable children to form abstractions from concrete experience.

The one problem with this theory is that, depending on prior learning or field of study, many older students and adults are not able to function at abstract levels. In certain circumstances, then, even adults still need concrete experience before they are able to use "abstract" verbal symbols as learning tools (Meyers, 1987, p. 29).

Vygotsky's contributions. More recently, Lev Vygotsky, the influential Russian developmental psychologist stressed the "essentially social nature of individual cognition" (Resnick, 1989, p. 396). According to Vygotsky, thinking begins as a social activity, but as individuals mature they internalize it. Finally, thinking reappears as an individual achievement.

Vygotsky believed that learning should be matched with a person's developmental status. He identified two aspects of development. The first aspect is the *actual developmental level*, determined by individual and independent problem solving. The second aspect is the *potential developmental level*, determined through problem solving under adult guidance or in collaboration with more capable peers. Vygotsky described the distance between these two levels as the *zone of proximal development*. Vygotsky's theory of social learning advanced the idea that social interaction creates zones of development that gradually become internalized and later become part of the person's independent developmental achievement (Brown & Palincscar, 1989).

Vygotsky—as well as Dewey and Piaget—recommended guided learning experience as an impetus to developmental change. The theories of cognition advanced by these thinkers all involved some form of internalization in social settings. The group setting provides a vehicle for eliciting clarification, justification, and elaboration from the learner. Vygotsky went further, however. He argued that what students do with the assistance of others was "even more indicative of their mental development than what they can do alone" (Resnick, 1989, p. 409).

Summary

Outdoor education has evolved and grown over the last 50 years in the schools. This growth came, in part, as a response to prevalent discontent with the confinement of learning to the two covers of a book, the four walls of a classroom, and the six separate subjects taught during distinct time periods in the school day.

Outdoor educators—among others interested in experiential education—wanted to move education beyond the 2 x 4 x 6 variety and into the community and surrounding area. The primary thrust of educational change occurred in the improvement of learning activities, teaching strategies, grouping arrangements, materials, and more effective use of instructional settings.

The idea of reflection is really quite common in some everyday areas of life, but not used very much by teachers in school situations. The use of reflection in outdoor learning has a great potential for expanding and clarifying meaning after a challenging outdoor activity, across many subject matter areas and grade levels. Reflection sessions also have great potential for improving experiential education in *any* setting (including the classroom). Indeed, without reflection learning becomes "inert."

Reflection is a process that usually follows experience, but it is known by several other terms. The other terms most often used by outdoor educators to indicate what this guidebook means by "reflection" are "debriefing" or "processing".

No matter what this part of the learning cycle is called, the literature reveals a substantial agreement among its advocates. Related terms that bear on reflection in important ways include "knowledge," "thinking," "experience," "learning," and "transfer." The words are simple, but the ideas they signify—and the relationships among those ideas—are complex. This guidebook offers one place to start exploring these relationships; but I suspect that the *experience* of conducting reflection sessions will lead you to new understandings and provide an incentive for further reading (and thinking, and action!).

Humans have been reflecting upon experience for many centuries, but only recently has the educational literature begun to consider the topic in depth and to refine the concept. Socrates, Dewey, Piaget, and Vygotsky were four thinkers who promoted the social aspects of reflecting upon experience in group settings. Educators are beginning to understand the value of constructing the meanings and interpreting the connections inherent in experience. Given the discovery that human beings are creatures who *must* make meaning and the recognition that real learning requires meaning-making, this change is an important one.

CHAPTER II

How to Lead a Reflection Session

As yet little research has been conducted on reflection in learning and that which has been undertaken offers few guidelines for the practical problems which face us as teachers and learners.
　　　　　　　　　　　　　—*Boud, Keogh, and Walker*
　　　　　Reflection: Turning Experience Into Learning

The absence of basic research is a problem, as the epigraph to this chapter indicates. Nonetheless, a growing body of writing based on action research and practical experience with reflection and metacognition strategies *does* exist.

Pearson and Smith (1988) believe that reflecting on (or "debriefing") an experience requires a range of specialized skills. They contend that such skills—especially those of interpersonal conduct and intervention in group processes, as well as those of timing—can be developed through training and refined through practice.

They believe that "the only way to learn to debrief is by doing it, and by watching others doing it with an attitude of deliberate and critical reflection" (Pearson & Smith, 1988, p. 83). They list six factors that contribute to effective debriefing:

(1) committing to its importance and central role in experience-based learning;

(2) deliberately planning for an adequate opportunity to reflect;

(3) realizing that a high level of facilitating skill is needed;

(4) establishing clear intentions, objectives, and purposes for all activities;

(5) identifying ways of knowing and types of knowledge that the experience represents and establishing appropriate structures and relationships in which the process will take place; and

(6) establishing an environment based upon trust, acceptance, risk taking, and mutual respect of individuals' feelings, perceptions, and theories.

We will examine each of these factors in more detail in this chapter by posing and answering six questions. This chapter concludes with a list of tips for conducting a reflection session. (Appendices A and B also list questions that should be considered as teachers probe deeper into the skills of leading reflection sessions.)

Why Is Reflection Important in Experience-Based Learning?

In order to learn from experience, we must take the time to sort the relevant from the irrelevant and the useful from the useless. After an experience, we can identify the important elements by asking, "What was significant to me?" Then we can analyze these elements in greater depth, considering the perspectives of both thinking and feeling. We can ask, "Why was this helpful or not helpful?" or "What did I feel when this happened?" Finally, we can generalize our thoughts and feelings in order to plan for the future. We can ask, "How will this be useful later?" or "When can this be applied to solve a similar problem?" (Appendix F provides additional questions to ask after participating in an instructional activity.)

Models of experience-based learning. Joplin (1981, p. 17) outlined a five-stage model of experiential education, based upon a review of the configuration of programs labeled "experiential." She concluded that experiential educators had two responsibilities in their program design: providing a challenging experience for the learner and facilitating reflection on that experience. According to Joplin (1981, p. 17), "Experience alone is insufficient to be called experiential education, and it is the reflection process which turns experience into experiential education."

The five-stage model is organized around a challenging action, preceded by a focus session and followed by a reflection (or "debriefing") session. Encompassing these three phases of the "action-reflection" cycle is an environment of support and feedback.

36

These five components - *focus, challenging action, debrief,* (with simultaneous *feedback* and *support*) form one full cycle, which begins again with another focus, challenging action, and debrief session.

Joplin believes that in the reflection phase, learning is recognized, articulated, and evaluated. Reflection in this setting sorts and orders information, and it often involves personal perceptions and beliefs. She strongly believes that the reflection phase needs to be made public through discussing, sharing of writing, or doing a project or presentation.

The Kolb, Rubin, and McIntyre model of the learning process emphasizes the importance of experience in a four-stage cycle (described in Boud et al., 1985). The stages are: immediate *concrete experience* as a basis for *observation and reflection,* which leads to the assimilation of observations into a theory consisting of *abstract concepts and generalizations* from which new implications or hypotheses are *tested in new situations.*

Kolb and colleagues believe that learners need four different kinds of abilities, which correspond to these stages, as follows: concrete experience abilities, reflective observation abilities, abstract conceptualization abilities, and active experimentation abilities (Boud et al., 1985). In terms of the model proposed by Kolb and colleagues, this guidebook is designed to help teachers expand the reflective observation ability of students.

Jones and Pfeiffer (1979) devised a five-step, cyclical process they describe as an experiential learning model. The cycle begins with involvement in the world (*experiencing*). The second step, *publishing,* is the sharing of observations, feelings, or other reactions (making them public in a group). The third step, *processing,* is a systematic examination of patterns and dynamics that emerge from the publication step. The next step, *generalizing,* takes the meanings that emerge from the previous step and relates them to life (the "so what?" of learning). In the final step, *applying,* these implications and principles are put to use to actual situations; the learner states how he or she will use the new learning or behavior. When the new learning or behavior is tested, the cycle begins again as a new experience. For more information about experiential learning cycles, see Palmer (1981).

Commonalities. The models briefly described above contain learning cycles with common elements. Each includes both an experience or action stage and a reflection ("debriefing" or "processing") stage. Teachers who accept any of these common experiential learning models must consider how to incorporate the reflection phase into their instruction and constantly strive to improve their skills in this area. The next section examines this challenge.

How Can I Deliberately Plan for a Reflection Session?

Obviously, teachers will not be able to control all the variables involved in outdoor experiences, but they can plan goals and objectives to guide their work. A teacher should be able to state clearly the reason for conducting a lesson outside the school building, or for that matter, in any particular setting. Whether the appropriate setting is indoors or out really depends on the nature of the planned experience (and ultimately on the nature of what is to be learned). Obviously, not everything that is usually taught indoors is most appropriately taught there. Similarly, not every activity taught outdoors is well thought-out.

Experienced teachers realize, of course, that not everything a student learns from a structured lesson can be anticipated. Nonetheless, we can still have our instructional sights aimed in a broad sense. We can clarify what we *intend* to accomplish, even if it is unwise to try to predict what *every* student will ultimately gain from the lesson.

Teachers also need to be flexible when they set objectives, especially outdoors, where "teachable moments" appear at every bend in the trail. Sometimes, plans *must* be scrapped in favor of a chance event that obviously captures the interest and excitement of students. Being flexible and "winging it" with an unforeseen circumstance is often the way to take advantage of the inherent motivation of many outdoor experiences.

In the instance of preparing questions ahead of time to help in the reflection phase, Gaw points out disadvantages as well as advantages. "One disadvantage is that the facilitator may come to rely solely on these questions without becoming knowledgeable about the concept, issue, or theory to be illuminated by the experience" (Gaw, 1979, p. 152).

Gaw (1979) also lists several advantages of preparing certain types of questions beforehand:

(1) If the experience *is* going as planned, the teacher can use the questions as tools to guide the pace, depth, and intensity deemed appropriate.

38

(2) If the experience *is not* going as planned, the teacher can still use some of the questions for deriving learning from what is going on.

As long as the prepared questions are viewed as tools to do a job, they can be used as is, or modified, if the situation changes. Gaw (1979, p. 152) concludes "that [the use of prepared] questions in themselves [is] neither good nor bad; it is how the facilitator uses them that is the object of evaluation."

A teacher could prepare for the reflection session by reviewing several structured exercises for possible use and making a list of them. This type of activity checklist can be applied in the same way that prepared questions are used or not used, depending upon the situation. The bottom line: Preparation usually helps to increase the probability that students will achieve planned objectives.

If the students view the reflection phase as useless and boring, however, no amount of teacher preparation will be effective. Even if a teacher approaches the reflection session with no prepared plan, he or she could conceivably turn the responsibility over to students—if they have come to value the reflection session. The important thing is for the teacher and the students to value setting aside some time to make sense out of the outdoor experience. Having the students "buy in" to reflecting is really the first step in implementing the experiential learning model.

How Can I Develop and Improve My Facilitation Skills?

If one believes that the student is ultimately the person who is in charge of his or her learning, the role of the teacher becomes more clear. Holding this view of education, the teacher's role becomes that of facilitating learning. According to Egan (1973, p. 33) "a 'facilitator' is one who offers whatever services he/she can to help others develop their own resources and talents."

This interpretation fits the original Latin meaning of the word, "educator" which is "to lead out" or "draw forth" knowledge from the student. Teachers who believe that students actively construct knowledge—the viewpoint of cognitive science—will understand that their role is to encourage (and "empower") students to take responsibility for their education.

To take this view, however, does not imply that teachers assume that all students will lead themselves to learning. Teachers are still responsible for establishing and working toward meaningful goals and objectives, usually in concert with the school and community.

They must have a plan, but they must also change their plans in accordance with feedback. Teachers must know when to intervene and when to stay quiet; when to lead and when to follow. Some of the teacher/facilitator roles are:

(1) convening of learning sessions;

(2) conducting "getting to know each other" activities;

(3) observing individual and group difficulties;

(4) supporting and maintaining a safe learning climate;

(5) enforcing agreed-upon norms and working guidelines;

(6) recommending challenging learning activities;

(7) leading group reflection on experiences;

(8) focusing upon mutually agreed upon goals and objectives;

(9) modeling recommended learning attitudes and behaviors;

(10) observing, listening, and evaluating; and

(11) summarizing and directing closure activities.

This list of roles is useless, however, if merely memorized, or if applied cookbook-fashion. Teachers need to develop an instructional style that is compatible with their beliefs about how we learn and what it means to educate. The listed roles are merely the sorts of things that come naturally to those who consider teaching as facilitating the work of students who actively construct meaning.

Caine and Caine (1991, p. 8) convey this idea through the use of the term "brain-based education." This idea, in their view, involves:

(1) designing and orchestrating lifelike, enriching, and appropriate experiences for learners and

(2) ensuring that students process experience in such a way as to increase the extraction of meaning.

The way to improve your own facilitation skills is an issue of individual learning style, but, in general, teachers need information, structure, and support to change the way they teach. This guidebook helps meet the first two needs. Support, however, can come from two sources: colleagues and students. My own experience with students is that the sort of teaching described throughout this guidebook wins the support of students. Networks of experiential and outdoor educators can also provide collegial support, even in the absence of local colleagues. Consult the Appendix for information about such resources.

Why Are Clear Intentions, Objectives, and Purposes Necessary?

As teachers we are usually hired to implement (and, on occasion, help to develop) the goals of the sponsoring agency, whether it be the school, church, camp, or outdoor center. Within these general limits, nonetheless, we and our students usually have a great deal of latitude

A snake in the hand is worth two in the field. (Photograph by Tom Lesser, Port Murray, NJ)

to choose how we will meet those goals, and, sometimes, even to add others based on our needs and interests.

If we don't know where we are going, we will never know if we get there. Here are a few possible destinations:

Facts, concepts, and principles. For example, we can go outside to find illustrations of the concept of "food chains". We can learn that the mouse-snake-owl relationship can be demonstrated in a snake having a mouse-like bulge mid-way along the slender body or signs of snake bones found in the regurgitated fur pellets from an owl. We can better understand the principle of predator and prey or how energy is lost as animals eat other animals.

Mental and physical skills. For example, the mental skill of problem solving can be demonstrated when students are given information about the aquatic organisms that are associated with different levels of water pollution. Then they can capture aquatic life with a net and determine whether or not the body of water is polluted. A physical skill, such as properly using a net or thermometer, can be taught and used to explore the aquatic environment. In many instances, physical and mental skills are combined and cannot be dealt with separately.

Attitudes and values. For example, the main goal of an outdoor lesson could be the development or clarification of an attitude or value about the outdoors. An attitude that we might want to instill in students is to allow snakes to continue to live because of the important niche they fill in the ecosystem. A broader and related value might be to respect all living things in the environment and to realize that living things have a right to life whether we need them or not. Some lessons can be directed towards attitudes and values as their main focus.

Task achievement. There are many tasks that can be considered goals of outdoor education activities. For example, constructing log steps along a trail, or getting the whole team over a twelve-foot wall, or picking up litter might be the tasks the group wants to accomplish. It is often easy to determine whether the task has been completed, but more difficult to pinpoint how to do it more efficiently and to a higher level of quality.

Process analysis. How the group works together in achieving tasks, or learning facts, concepts, principles, mental and physical skills, or attitudes and values can be the major focus. Process analysis involves individual personal abilities such as being aware of feelings, affirming personal worth, demonstrating a sense of humor, taking appropriate risks, accepting feedback non-defensively, or identifying personal needs and wants. It also involves certain interpersonal abilities such as communicating thoughts and feelings, empathizing with others, interpreting nonverbal language, complimenting others, trusting the group, dealing effectively with conflict, or cooperating with others.

These possible destinations obviously have a good deal to do with reflection. Mezirow, however, describes five types of reflectivity (cited in Boud et al., 1985, p. 25) that are relevant to where reflection sessions might go. Each of these types can serve as goals for planning reflection strategies, as follows:

(1) **affective**—becoming aware of how we feel about the way we are perceiving, thinking or acting;

(2) **discriminant**—assessing the efficacy of our perceptions, thoughts, actions, and habits of doing things;

(3) **judgmental**—becoming aware of our value judgements about our perceptions, thoughts, actions, and habits;

(4) **conceptual**—being conscious of our awareness of constructs; and

(5) **psychic**—making assessments about people on the basis of limited information.

Unless the teacher is clear about why the students are participating in the outdoor activity, it is difficult to lead a structured reflection activity. The preceding lists will help you think about your objectives for a particular reflection session.

How Can Ways of Knowing and Types of Knowledge Guide Reflection?

At this point, you may wish to re-read and review the earlier section, "What is Knowledge and Knowing?" (see pp. 17). These distinctions are critical in planning reflection sessions.

Understanding the differences among "know-that" (declarative) knowledge, "know-how" (procedural) knowledge, and conditional knowledge, you can select a structured reflection strategy that fits the type of knowledge your lesson seeks to cultivate. Understanding how natural knowledge differs from surface or inert knowledge, you can guide learning more directly during the reflection session. Similarly, identifying generative knowledge will help you ask students to examine new information in relation to previously held information. We can help students assess their present knowledge schemas and incorporate new learnings into what already exists. Finally, with an appreciation of Gardner's knowledge domains (intelligences), you can more clearly understand what may be happening with individuals (whose strengths vary).

How Can We Help Establish a Community Climate That Supports Reflection?

> *I never teach my pupils; I only attempt to provide the conditions in which they can learn.*
> —*Albert Einstein*, Experiential Learning and Change *(Walter & Marks, 1981)*

If we follow Einstein's lead, we can consciously attempt to create a climate based on trust, acceptance, appropriate risk taking, and mutual respect for others. Walter and Marks (1981, p. 7) define climate "as the atmosphere or the general tone of the learning experience." A defensive climate inhibits learning. The elements of defensive climate include evaluation, control, strategy, neutrality, superiority, and certainty. According to them,

> An emphasis on evaluation, control, and the assertion of superiority tends to evoke anxiety and competitive feelings in participants. Strategy breeds suspicion and fear of unfairness; certainty denies individuals the opportunity to participate in the determination of events and devalues their perceptions. Neutrality implies minimized mutual commitment among individuals.
>
> (Walter & Marks, 1981, p. 7)

Supportive climate. A supportive climate is different. Some teachers manage to create such a climate. These teachers

• describe events—rather than enforcing continuous evaluation of ongoing events,

• encourage students to consider problems—rather than trying to control everything,

44

- maintain a spontaneous and flexible approach—rather than having every detail planned,

- develop feelings of empathy toward students—rather than being neutral or "objective,"

- project a tone of equality (with the attitude that "We're all in this learning adventure together")—rather than projecting an air of superiority, and

- show a tendency toward provisionalism or experimentation—rather than certainty.

Howard, Howell, and Brainard (1987, p. 6-11) note that a positive climate must provide for essential human needs: *physiological* (warmth, light, and space needs); *safety* (both physical and psychological security); *acceptance and friendship* (closeness with everyone involved); *achievement and recognition* (acknowledging successes); and *maximizing potential* (to the highest degree possible by each person). Howard and colleagues identified eight factors that contribute to positive climate: continuous academic and social growth, respect, trust, high morale, cohesiveness, opportunities for input, renewal, and caring. They also report that a supportive climate depends on the presence of productive group dynamics and suitable instructional and environmental materials.

A caring community of learners. Another way to cultivate a supportive climate is to create a caring community of learners. "Community building" is a process by which some groups achieve this end. It involves a gradual succession of stages, beginning with a collection of individuals and progressing to a closely-knit group in which members identify with one another and share common values and goals. In short, the group develops an identity.

Although members of such a community share a set of core values and knowledge, they also respect the diversity within the group. Caring communities function with a set of agreed-upon standards of behavior of a sort that enable the members to cooperate, trust, communicate, and care about each other. Community members recognize that everyone wants to feel—and to be—included in the group identity. But such communities also have the potential to expand their feelings of unity, regress to former stages, or split up completely. A caring community is strong (because it cares) and

Reflecting upon an outdoor experience can expand meaning for everyone. (Photograph by George Tarbay, Art-Photo Dept., Northern Illinois University)

fragile (because maintaining such a community takes work) at the same time. It shares this circumstance with other caring human relationships.

Community-building skills are important to learn and practice because:

(1) people have a basic need to belong to social groups;

(2) people working together are better able to solve problems and make wise decisions that improve their environment;

(3) groups help most people learn and retain concepts and information in ways that are not otherwise possible;

(4) democracy requires cooperation; and

46

(5) groups are the best context in which to master personal and interpersonal skills.

The most important foundation of a caring community is the desire of all its members to build and maintain the community structure. The building blocks of a caring community consist of personal attitudes and beliefs about interpersonal skills. Here are some of the most important ones:

- I believe in the value of people and their abilities to resolve conflicts constructively.

- I want to be recognized and praised for my inner goodness and accomplishments if your praise is genuine.

- I need you and others, and I value your support and encouragement.

- Your trust for me can grow when I earn it through my positive interactions with you.

- When I am open and truthful with you about who I really am, you will grow to respect me more.

- It is worthwhile to limit some of my freedoms for the good of the whole community.

- I can disagree with your opinions, but still accept you as a valuable person.

- If I attempt to see the world from your perspective and listen to you attentively, I may understand you better.

- Having a clear purpose for our community and knowing how to reach our goals helps me feel more effective and in control of my life.

- Knowing and accepting the rules and norms for operating in this community helps to reduce conflicts and resolve problems.

There is no substitute for openly and honestly discussing the creation of a caring community of learners. Often, the group may want to construct a set of guidelines and norms that promote a supportive climate. Here is one example:

Because I believe in the importance of a caring community, I agree to:

(1) preserve confidentiality by respecting the privacy of the group members;

(2) participate in the group activities as much as possible until the end of the experience;

(3) ask for what I want and need, but not expect to get all I ask for;

(4) speak only for myself and not others;

(5) stay in the "here and now" as much as possible, rather than deal with other groups and other times;

(6) express my feelings in ways that will show my respect for the dignity of individuals;

(7) take appropriate risks as my trust for the group increases;

(8) stay in touch with my internal talk and learn from it whenever I can;

(9) decide on how I want to be different as a result of this experience and develop a plan for changing;

(10) be open and honest with the group members;

(11) be silent when it feels right; and

(12) treat the group members with respect, even if I don't agree with their behavior.

Appendix D provides a checklist ("Checking for a Sense of Community") for you and your students to examine, both now and in the future. Appendix E consists of seven quetions to help you and your students reflect upon the experience of using the checklist presented in Appendix D.

Leading a Reflection Session

Throughout this guidebook, I assume that you share two beliefs with me: (1) learning is not limited to the classroom and (2) helping students make meaning is what education is all about. I also assume that many readers will not yet have had the experience of consciously planning to conduct a reflection session. The purpose of this chapter is to help *you* begin to construct the web of ideas related to leading a reflection session, or to say it another way: to help you make your own meaning.

It should be obvious to you by now that I don't highly value "cookbook" education. At the same time, we all have to start somewhere. I offer the following tips in this spirit. Remember—these are just pointers that come from my own experience and reflection. They are not rules. Rather, these tips represent some of the sense I have made of my experience. They may benefit experienced outdoor educators and teachers who have led reflection sessions, as well as neophytes. But they do not represent a sure-fire "recipe" for success. Teachers, as well as students, vary. As you review the list, then, reflect on who you are and how you work best.

Tips for Leading a Reflection Session
(Adapted from Knapp, 1990, p. 196)

(1) Select the educational objectives appropriate for the students participating in the outdoor experience and those that you are qualified to address.

(2) Whenever possible, share the educational objectives with the students at an appropriate time in the lesson.

(3) If the group is not well known to you, find out as much as possible about the group before planning the outdoor activities and establishing a plan for reflecting on the experience.

(4) Allow an adequate length of time to reflect upon the individual components of the total experience.

(5) Share the expected ground rules and group norms of behavior with the students. If time permits, involve them in developing these ground rules and norms.

(6) Stress the importance of maintaining confidentiality

49

among members of the group, especially on sensitive personal and interpersonal issues.

(7) Respect a student's right to remain silent or "pass" during the reflection session, but recognize that students always need to be given ample opportunities to interact verbally with others in a safe environment.

(8) Respond to students in ways that demonstrate a high regard for their abilities and self-concept.

(9) Take the time to help the students consider ways of applying new learnings in other settings in the future.

(10) Convey the idea that students are ultimately responsible for their own learning and that reflection sessions are designed to help them get the most from experience.

(11) Be aware of student attitudes toward the reflection session by "reading" their verbal and nonverbal reactions. Do not persist in the session if a majority of students are uncomfortable. Confront the group about how they are feeling and either change direction or stop the reflection session when discomfort becomes too great.

(12) Verbally and nonverbally compliment students who make insightful contributions to the reflection session. The teacher can encourage students in building a positive climate for reflection.

(13) If certain students dominate the outdoor activity or the reflection session, tactfully find ways of involving more of the silent students without insulting the dominators.

(14) Do not feel that you must lead a reflection session after each activity, but do not allow too much time to pass before asking students to recall and comment upon an activity.

(15) Do not hesitate, once in a while, to offer your own observations of what you saw happening in the group. Be careful, however, not to dominate the talk time at the expense of student talk.

(16) Be attentive to the physical arrangement of the group while conducting the reflection session. The best arrangement is one in which everyone can see faces and hear comments.

(17) Feel free to take notes during the outdoor activity so that you will remember important comments or events. A 3" X 5" card held in the hand or kept in a pocket works well.

(18) Develop ways to encourage student-to-student talk rather than always having the invitation for discussion come from you.

(19) Sometimes a reflection session works best when students can speak spontaneously rather than raise their hands. Structure the session, however, so that the quiet—or more reserved—students have ample opportunities to speak.

(20) Explain the difference between the group task (e.g., netting aquatic life, finding a tree explored while blindfolded, or climbing a 12-foot wall) and the objective of the lesson, which might be something different. If this distinction is made clear, students could "fail" to accomplish the task, but succeed in reaching the lesson objective.

(21) As a general rule, attempt to structure sessions in such a way as to move from low threat to higher threat and from the concrete situation to more general or abstract applications.

Summary

This chapter examined six main aspects of effective leadership for reflection sessions. Such leadership requires teachers who are committed to the importance of experiential education and convinced of the central role of reflection. Reflection sessions must be planned, of course, and this planning must ensure that experiences (that is, outdoor activities) themselves are planned so as to permit time for structured reflection.

Teachers must recognize that an adequate level of facilitation skill is needed to get the most from the reflection session. Self-knowledge is important. Teachers must be aware of their own skill levels and not

Learning the skills of canoeing is a good example of "know-how."
(Photograph by Northern Illinois University Art/Photo, Dekalb, IL)

venture too deeply into areas that they don't have the expertise to handle effectively.

Teachers must enter into the reflection session clearly aware of why they structured a particular activity and how they intend to direct the expansion and clarification of its meaning with students. At the same time, they need to be flexible enough to modify the planned goals and change direction. Related to intentions, objectives, and purposes of the session, are the different ways and degrees of knowing, since advancing knowledge is the main reason for teaching. Teachers need to distinguish what kinds of knowledge they are working with during a reflection session.

Finally, teachers must plan for and take the time to deal with the task of building a supportive community climate. The lack of a supportive community climate will compromise their ability to lead an effective reflection session. One can begin modestly by developing ground rules with a group of students who have not previously worked together. Over time, the development of a supportive community will improve the meanings students construct during reflection sessions.

CHAPTER III

Developing the Art and Science of Questioning

I came to appreciate that the right question is usually more important than the right answers to the wrong question.
— *Alvin Toffler*, The Third Wave

Questioning strategies are powerful tools in the reflection process. Both students and teachers can pose questions to the group in order to expand their personal meanings of experiences. Socrates used the question as a way of uncovering truth to such an extent that educators credited him for originating this strategy. Bitting and Clift (1988, p. 11) note that

> According to Socrates, knowledge was to be sought within the mind and brought to birth by questioning. He contrasts perceiving, or the observation of things outside oneself, with *reflection*, the discovery of what is within, an activity he held to be common to both mathematics and ethics.

According to Paul and Binker (1990, p. 269), the purpose of Socratic questioning is to help "students...synthesize their beliefs into a more coherent and better-developed perspective."

Listening to students is an important first step before constructing effective probing questions. This approach is based on the idea that all thinking has a logic—or inherent structure—and that a statement reveals only one piece of a system of interconnected beliefs (Paul & Binker, 1990). Probing provides a way to help students become self-correcting instead of depending upon the teacher to correct mistaken ideas.

Brown and Palincsar (1989, p. 411) describe Socratic dialogue, or discovery teaching, as a theory of instruction. They suggest that this method has a three-part goal, to achieve (a) facts and concepts, (b) rules or theories to account for these concepts, and (c) methods for deriving rules or theories in general. These goals are accomplished by encouraging students to elaborate, justify, and provide supportive evidence for their statements.

Five main discussion ploys are used:

(1) systematic variation of cases (e.g.," Do you behave the same way in other groups?"),

(2) counter examples and hypothetical cases (e.g., "Would you say that if the group was made up of all boys?"),

(3) entrapment strategies (e.g., "Do you believe that all girls think the same way on that issue?"),

(4) hypothesis identification strategies (e.g., "Why do you think some group members couldn't keep quiet during this silent walk?"), and

(5) hypothesis evaluation strategies (e.g., "How many would agree with John's explanation of why the group acted that way?").

Brown and Palincsar (1989, p. 412) claim that Socratic questioning is valuable because it models scientific thought and therefore teaches students to think critically. Another advantage of the method is that it allows the teacher to question students on their levels of understanding or misunderstanding, thereby serving as a way of assessing how well students realize the objective of the lesson. Another obvious benefit is the high degree of student involvement in the learning process. This way of attending to students often produces high levels of motivation.

Paul and Binker (1990, pp. 271-275) describes three basic forms of Socratic questioning: the spontaneous, the exploratory, and the issue-specific. Each is considered, next.

Spontaneous questioning. It might appear contradictory to say that a spontaneous questioning session can be planned. However, a teacher can prepare by becoming familiar with some generic Socratic questions and practicing these question types until they feel comfortable. Teachers can, for example, ask:

- for evidence (e.g., "What made you say that Susie was scared?"),

- for reasons to explain behavior (e.g., "Why was it difficult to ask for what you needed?"),

- for examples (e.g., "Can you think of other ways the boys took charge?"),

- other students if they agree (e.g., "John, do you agree with Pam that the group is not working well together?"),

- for analogous or parallel cases (e.g., "Phil, have you ever seen our group have trouble listening to each other in school?"),

- for paraphrases of opposing views (e.g., "Can anyone state the two different points that have been expressed?"), or

- questions that rephrase student responses (e.g., "Mary, did I hear you say that you felt proud of how you helped solve this group problem?").

By attending to such question types as these, teachers can develop the skill of guiding an emerging discussion. Indeed, such skill is critically important to helping students probe unexpected events for hidden meanings or helping them deal with issues not foreseen in the lesson plan. By responding to students' statements with probing questions, teachers can help create a norm that supports a sharing of ideas and a mutual search for the truth. (For additional generic questions, see Appendices F and G.)

Exploratory questioning. The purpose of this form of questioning is to survey what the students think and feel on a variety of topics. The teacher can assess the students' abilities to express themselves, their value positions, and where their thinking is clear or fuzzy. The teacher can uncover areas of disagreement or interest. This form can serve as a way of finding out "where they are" before charting the instructional path to get there.

The teacher can prepare for exploratory questioning by predicting the issues that might arise from an activity and then writing some relevant questions for each one. The teacher might also predict student responses to these questions and prepare follow-up probes. Teachers can never be sure how the session will unfold and therefore, it is impossible to anticipate all of the appropriate questions beforehand.

When cooperative learning is used as the strategy to explore a topic, teachers can predict that certain problems of group dynamics will arise and prepare questions to find out which ones apply to the group. Some possible topics are: communication problems, difficulty in expressing feelings, critical judgment of others, inability to make decisions, and unwillingness to trust the group members. (See Appendix J for sample questions to ask.)

Issue-specific questioning. This form of Socratic questioning is designed to probe an issue or concept in depth in order to clarify, analyze, and evaluate it. Teachers can prepare by identifying issues that seem relevant to the group or activity, then thinking through various dimensions of them. If the teacher knows the group well, the student responses to the questions might also be predicted and planned for.

Although issues specific to content relate to the experience planned, human relations issues surface in all group work. The following questions concern human relations issues across the full range of cooperative activities (adapted from Knapp, 1984, pp. 47-49). (For examples of questions to consider following a particular activity—an outdoor solo experience—see Appendices H and I.)

- **Communicating Effectively.**

  (1) Can anyone give an example of when you thought you communicated effectively with someone else in the group? (Consider verbal and non-verbal communication.)

  (2) How did you know that what you communicated was understood? (Consider different types of feedback.)

  (3) Who didn't understand someone's attempt to communicate?

  (4) What went wrong in the communication attempt?

  (5) What could the communicator do differently next time to give a clearer message?

  (6) What could the message receiver do differently next time to understand the message?

  (7) How many different ways were used to communicate messages?

56

(8) Which ways were most effective? Why?

(9) Did you learn something about communication that will be helpful later? If so, what?

- Expressing appropriate feelings.

    (1) Can you name a feeling you had at any point in completing the activity (for example consider mad, glad, sad, or scared)? Where in your body did you feel it most?

    (2) What personal beliefs were responsible for generating that feeling? What was the main thought behind the feeling?

    (3) Is that feeling a common one in your life?

    (4) Did you express that feeling to others? If not, what did you do with the feeling?

    (5) Do you usually express feelings or suppress them?

    (6) Would you like to feel differently in a similar situation? If so, how would you like to feel?

    (7) What beliefs would you need to have in order to feel differently in a similar situation? Could you believe them?

    (8) How do you feel about the conflict that may result from expressing certain feelings?

    (9) How do you imagine others felt toward you at various times during the activity? Were these feelings expressed?

    (10) What types of feelings are easiest to express?...most difficult?

    (11) Do you find it difficult to be aware of some feelings at times? If so, which ones?

    (12) Are some feelings not appropriate to express to the group at times? If so, which ones?

    (13) What feelings were expressed nonverbally in the group?

    (14) Does expressing appropriate feelings help or hinder completing the task?

- **Deferring judgment of others.**

    (1) Is it difficult for you to avoid judging others? Explain.

    (2) Can you think of examples of when you judged others in the group today?...when you didn't judge others?

    (3) What were some advantages to you of not judging others?

    (4) What were some advantages to others of your not judging them?

    (5) How does judging and not judging others affect the completion of the activity?

    (6) Were some behaviors of others easy not to judge and other behaviors difficult?

    (7) Would deferring judgment be of some value in other situations? Explain.

    (8) Can you think of any disadvantages of not judging others in this situation?

- **Listening.**

    (1) Who made suggestions for completing the activity?

    (2) Were all of these suggestions heard? Explain.

    (3) Which suggestions were acted upon?

    (4) Why were the other suggestions ignored?

    (5) How did it feel to be heard when you made a suggestion?

    (6) What interfered with your ability to listen to others?

    (7) How can this interference be overcome?

    (8) Did you prevent yourself from listening well? How?

    (9) Did you listen in the same way today as you generally do? If not, what was different about today?

- **Leading others.**

  (1) Who assumed leadership roles during the activity?

  (2) What were the behaviors that you described as showing leadership?

  (3) Can everyone agree that these behaviors are traits of leaders?

  (4) How did the group respond to these leadership behaviors?

  (5) Who followed the leader even if unsure that the idea would work? Why?

  (6) Did the leadership role shift to other people during the activity? Who thought they were taking the leadership role? How did you do it?

  (7) Was it difficult to assume a leadership role with this group?

  (8) Why didn't some of you take a leadership role?

  (9) Is it easier to take a leadership role in other situations or with different group members? Explain.

  (10) Did anyone try to lead the group, but felt they were unsuccessful? What were some possible reasons for this? How did it feel to be disregarded?

- **Following others.**

  (1) Who assumed a follower role at times throughout the activity? How did it feel?

  (2) How did it feel to follow different leaders?

  (3) Do you consider yourself a good follower? Was this an important role in the group today? Explain.

  (4) How does refusal to follow affect the leadership role?

  (5) What are the traits of a good follower?

  (6) How can you improve your ability to follow in the future?

- **Making group decisions.**

    (1) How were group decisions made in completing the activity?

    (2) Were you satisfied with the ways decisions were made? Explain.

    (3) Did the group arrive at any decisions through group consensus? (Some didn't get their first choice, but they could "live" with the decision.)

    (4) Were some decisions made by one or by several individuals?

    (5) Did everyone in the group express an opinion when a choice was available? If not, why not?

    (6) What is the best way for this group to make decisions? Explain.

    (7) Do you respond in similar ways in other groups?

    (8) What did you like about how the group made decisions? What didn't you like?

- **Cooperating.**

    (1) Can you think of specific examples of when the group cooperated in completing the activity? Explain.

    (2) How did it feel to cooperate?

    (3) Do you cooperate in most things you do?

    (4) How did you learn to cooperate?

    (5) What are the rewards of cooperating?

    (6) Are there any problems associated with cooperation?

    (7) How did cooperative behavior lead to completing the activity successfully?

    (8) How can you cooperate in other areas of your life?

    (9) Did you think anyone was blocking the group from cooperating? Explain.

- **Respecting human differences.**

    (1) How are you different from some of the others in the group?

    (2) How do these differences strengthen the group as a whole?

    (3) When do differences in people in a group prevent reaching certain objectives?

    (4) What would this group be like if there were very few differences in people? How would you feel if this were so?

    (5) In what instances did being different help and hinder the group members from reaching their objectives?

- **Respecting human commonalities.**

    (1) How are you like some of the others in the group?

    (2) Were these commonalities a help to the group in completing their task? Explain.

    (3) Were these commonalities a hinderance to the group in completing their task? Explain.

    (4) Do you think you have other things in common with some of the group members, but that you haven't found yet?

    (5) How did this setting help you discover how you are similar to others?

- **Trusting the group.**

    (1) Can you give examples of when you trusted someone in the group? Explain.

    (2) Is it easier to trust some people and not others? Explain.

    (3) Can you think of examples when trusting someone would not have been a good idea?

    (4) How do you increase your level of trust for someone?

    (5) On a scale from 1-10, rate how much trust you have in the group as a whole. Can you explain your rating?

(6)   What did you do today that deserves the trust of others?

(7)   How does the amount of fear you feel affect your trust of others?

Hierarchies of Questions

Paul and Binker (1990, pp. 276-277) list six categories of questions and provide examples of each:

*   questions of clarification (e.g., "What do you mean by _____?");

*   questions that probe assumptions (e.g., "What is Daren assuming?");

*   questions that probe reasons and evidence (e.g., "Why do you think that is true?");

*   questions about viewpoints or perspectives (e.g., "Why have you chosen this rather than that perspective?")

*   questions that probe implications and consequences (e.g., "What effect would that have?"); and

*   questions about the question (e.g., "How can we find out?").

These categories have a great deal to do with the kinds of questions illustrated in the preceding consideration of discussion strategies. But questions can also be categorized hierarchically, from simple to complex.

According to Dantonio (1990, p. 16), questioning hierarchies and categorization systems flourish in the literature. She describes four major systems of classifying questions. Each is summarized briefly in the following discussion. Readers should consider the features of each and investigate further those that appeal most to their styles of teaching—or to the learning styles of their students.

Bloom's taxonomies. Bloom's system for determining the cognitive levels of objectives can also serve to guide the types of questions a teacher might ask. Bloom's major categories—familiar to most teachers—are: knowledge, comprehension, application, analysis, synthesis, and evaluation.

One problem in using this system to frame questions is that the student may not respond on the same cognitive level that the question was designed to probe. In other words, if a teacher asks a question

The art of questioning students on a log can be practiced as Socrates and his students did years ago. (Photograph by George Tarbay, Art-Photo Dept., Northern Illinois University)

designed to require a student to combine certain observations and draw a generalization from them (synthesize), a student may simply recall some facts (at the knowledge level) and respond to the question using that information. Part of this difficulty is the fact that classroom instructional routines are most often based on knowledge-level questions. Experiential educators, with a rich view of reflection, therefore, will most likely need to help students develop their abilities to provide the more elaborate responses that higher-order cognitive questions require. To help students, therefore, teachers may need to ask a series of probe questions.

Bloom did not confine his taxonomic work to the cognitive domain, however. He was also part of a group of psychologists who developed a taxonomy of educational goals in the affective domain (Krathwohl, Bloom, & Masia, 1956). This taxonomy is less familiar than Bloom's taxonomy in the cognitive domain. Teachers can, however, devise questions to correspond with the following levels of the affective continuum:

(1) receiving or attending to a phenomenon (at the increasing intensity levels of awareness, willingness to receive, and selected attention),

63

(2) responding to a phenomenon (at the increasing intensity levels of complying with encouragement, willingness to respond, and responding with satisfaction),

(3) valuing a phenomenon (at the increasing intensity levels of acceptance, preference, and commitment),

(4) organization of a value into a system (at the increasing intensity levels of conceptualization and ordered relationship of several related values), and

(5) organization into a value complex (at the increasing intensity levels of incorporating values into a set of unique personal characteristics and a philosophy of life).

The last level is difficult to assess in schools because it usually occurs after students have graduated from formal educational institutions. Some examples of questions at each of the four main levels of the affective continuum follow:

(1) receiving: John, did you realize that Mary felt left out?

(2) responding: Tania, how did you feel when you came up with the solution to the problem?

(3) valuing: Phyllis, you seem to really believe in cooperating rather than competing. Is that true?

(4) organization: Bob, can you give some examples of how you have lived a nonviolent life?

Aschner-Gallagher's question system. This system is based on Guilford's Structure of the Intellect model. The Aschner-Gallagher system has four categories: cognitive memory, convergent, divergent, and valuative questions.

The first category requires rote memory and factual recall. Convergent questions require a type of thinking that usually results in single right or wrong response, based on supportive information. Divergent questions require generating new information and making predictions to solve problems, often with more than one correct answer. Valuative questions require students to make judgments based on certain criteria.

Obvious parallels exist between the Bloom hierarchies and the Aschner-Gallagher system. In both schemes, factual recall (or "knowledge" in the Bloom model) constitutes the simplest, and is elicited by the most basic form of question. Similarly, judgment comes into play when students respond to the most complex, or elaborate, questions. In distinguishing between convergent and divergent questions, however, the latter model distinguishes between the kinds of questions for which "right" answers exist and those that require teachers and students to consider what may—or may not—be appropriate in a response (i.e., "divergent" questions).

Taba's instructional systems. Unlike the previous two systems, Taba considers the *sequencing* of questions in her instructional systems. Whereas one may, for example in the Bloom taxonomies, intersperse the various levels of questions more or less randomly, Taba understands that—in the instructional setting—the sequencing of questions is important. Thus, Taba develops models in which the order of teacher questions becomes important.

The Taba thought systems are: concept development, interpretation of data, and application of a generalization. Concept development is a questioning sequence designed to develop, refine, and extend concepts. Interpreting data requires knowledge of concepts and focuses on cause-and-effect relationships. Questions in this sequence emphasize evidence and reasoning in arriving at generalizations. The application of a generalization sequence enables students to solve problems by explaining unfamiliar phenomena or predicting consequences from known conditions.

Hyman's classified questions. Hyman devised the following types of questions: definitional, empirical, valuative, and metaphysical. Definitional questions ask students to define words or phrases. Empirical questions ask students to compare and contrast, draw inferences from information, or use other ways to analyze data. Valuative questions require the use of judgments, whereas metaphysical questions require students to do abstract thinking or make theoretical assumptions.

Applying Knowledge of Question Types

Dantonio (1990, p. 16) cited research concluding that merely knowing these various ways of classifying questions will not necessarily improve the way in which teachers ask questions.

Dantonio noted that questioning skills cannot be developed by simply reading about them. She, therefore, recommends a four-part "Talent Development Model" in which teachers (1) study the theory and rationale of a teaching strategy, (2) observe an expert demonstrate the strategy, (3) practice and receive feedback on performance in a safe environment, and (4) use peer coaching as a means of helping improve performance in instructional settings.

Such a program, in fact, is undergoing development at the Appalachia Educational Laboratory (AEL). The "QUILT" program ("Questioning and Understanding to Improve Learning and Thinking") trains teachers in the range of skills needed to ask better questions for improving students' thinking and discussion. The skills taught are those identified as effective by current research, and Bloom's cognitive taxonomy figures prominently in program activities. The QUILT materials are currently being used by about 1,200 classroom teachers, and an evaluation of program effects is underway. For further information, contact Sandra Orletsky at AEL (1-800/624-9120 nationally, or 1-800/344-6646 in West Virginia).

Awareness of different ways to categorize questions, then, is just a beginning point for change. In the absence of access to formal training programs, however, teachers who operate on the assumptions underlying this guidebook can still take steps on their own to improve how they ask questions.

Gaw (1979), for instance, suggests preparing a list of questions that coincide with each stage of Pfeiffer and Jones' experiential learning cycle (experiencing, sharing, interpreting, generalizing, and applying). She also adds another stage, described as processing the entire experience, and she prepares an additional set of questions designed to solicit feedback from the students. Here are some examples from each of the six categories:

(1) **Experiencing**

- What is going on?
- Would you be willing to try?
- Would you say more about that?

(2) **Sharing**

- What went on or what happened?
- How did you feel about that?
- Who else had the same experience?

(3) **Interpreting**

- How did you account for that?

- What does that mean to you?
- How do those fit together?

(4) Generalizing

- What did you learn or relearn?
- How does this relate to other experiences?
- What do you associate with that?

(5) Applying

- How could you apply or transfer that?
- What would you like to do with that?
- How could you make it better?

(6) Processing the entire experience

- How was this for you?
- What were the pluses/minuses
- If you had it to do over again, what would you do?

Glenn and Nelson (1989, pp. 55-56) present another system for helping students expand their perceptions of experience. They describe four levels through which learning passes: (1) the experience itself, (2) what we identify as significant in that experience, (3) our analysis, based on reason, of why it is significant, and (4) our generalization about the future value of the experience.

They suggest that these elements can be remembered by asking the questions, "What?", "Why?", and "How?" For example:

After the experience, we can ask:

- What happened?

- What did you see?

- What are you feeling?

- What was the most important thing?

Then we can help students analyze why aspects of the event were important by asking:

- Why was that significant to you?

- Why do you think it happened?

And finally, we can help them find a principle that may be useful in similar situations by asking:

- How can you use this information in the future?
- How can you do it differently next time for different results?

Glenn and Nelson (1989, p. 56) conclude, "One of the most common errors in working with young people is to assume that they understand and interpret what they experience as a mature person would."

Tips for Better Questioning

Although this guidebook cannot replace the practicing of questioning skills in group settings, it does provide some basic information and it offers suggestions for practice. The following tips are intended to help teachers improve their questioning strategies. Whereas I developed the tips that concluded the previous chapter from my own experience, the tips that follow represent the findings of educational research (e.g., Dantonio, 1990; Rowe, 1987), though they also accord well with my own experience.

(1) The phrasing of questions must be clear and concise. They should: (a) contain words that are easily understood, (b) not be cluttered with additional questions or explanations, (c) focus students on the content, and (d) identify the specific thinking skill students are to use in answering the question.

(2) The teacher should wait an appropriate length of time after asking the question and again before responding to the students' answers. This technique is known as "wait time" and will improve the quality of student responses. "Wait time 1" is the time that elapses *before* the student responds to the question posed. The recommended period for wait time 1 is 3-5 seconds or longer. (Research has shown that traditionally teachers pause less than one second.) "Wait time 2" is the time provided for thinking *after* the student answers the question. The additional 3-5 seconds will allow a student to elaborate or modify a response without being cut off by the teacher.

(3) Follow-up questions should be asked to seek clarification, sharpen awareness, or refine previous responses. Attention to follow-up questions can expand the learning for others in the group, as well as the person being questioned.

(4) Using the different classification systems of question types, be aware of how your questions vary. Try to use a variety of questions rather than focus on one type only. Research suggests that about 60 percent of teachers' questions focus on factual recall, about 20 percent require students to think, and the remaining 20 concern classroom procedures.

(5) Avoid the trap of accepting only the one "right" answer you, as the teacher, have in mind. Repeated asking of questions with the sole purpose of reproducing the teacher's answer cuts off discussion, prevents elaboration of ideas, and, ultimately, prevents thought. In short, include many divergent questions in your instructional routine.

(6) Be careful not to tip off the student as to the answer you expect or value. An acceptable response to the question, "We don't solve the problem by hitting, do we?" is seldom, "Yes."

(7) Listen carefully to student responses. Better questions can be asked if student responses are listened to and really heard. Resist the temptation to believe that students know only what they say. If in doubt, probe.

(8) Address questions to the whole group if everyone can benefit from thinking about them. You can always re-focus a question and direct it to specific students after giving the whole group a chance to think about it. Identify students who rarely offer an answer to these types of questions, and then be sure to target them specifically, from time to time.

(9) Encourage students to ask questions at appropriate times. In some cases, they may ask more probing and insightful questions than you are able to think of at the moment. Respect students' insights and welcome tough questions from them.

(10) Use your planned objectives as the guide for developing a sequence of questions, but be willing to abandon preset objectives and establish others spontaneously, if you observe events that warrant such a change.

(11) Encourage students to speak loudly enough so that everyone can hear the responses. Students' need to learn that their answers are just as important as your questions.

Summary

In 1945 Wertheimer (p. 123) noted that "often in great discovery the most important thing is that a certain question be found." This insight is especially important in reflection sessions. After all, the purpose of such sessions is to help students discover what they have learned and construct meaning. Appropriate questioning techniques are essential.

The skill of devising effective questions is a combination of art and science. The fine points of sequencing, timing, and selecting questions cannot be prescribed in cookbook fashion, nor can the skill of applying such fine points be learned only by reading or listening to lectures. This chapter, however, provides a beginning point for teachers who want to develop their questioning skills through study and practice.

History credits Socrates with developing the art and science of questioning in order to advance knowledge and discover truth. Socrates, however, apparently did not examine the skill of questioning with the sort of scrutiny the topic receives today. Since his day, however, others built on the foundation provided by his example. Today, there is little doubt that questioning is a powerful instructional tool for guiding reflection.

This chapter provided various forms of Socratic questioning, together with some examples that apply to outdoor teaching in particular. Other educators such as Paul and Binker, Bloom, Aschner and Gallagher, Taba, Hyman, and Gaw offer alternative ways of organizing and categorizing questions. The checklists provided in this chapter, however, are perhaps most useful as reminders that there are many ways to ask questions and many purposes toward which to direct them. The chapter ends with some tips for teachers to help them ask better questions.

CHAPTER IV

Alternative Activities for Reflecting

The most widely used strategy for conducting a reflection session consists of the teacher posing carefully selected and sequenced questions to which students respond, as a whole group, in smaller groups, or as individuals. This strategy is effective from the standpoint of sharing in the total learning community. The one drawback is that whole-group reflection sessions make it more difficult to ensure that everyone in the group verbalizes thoughts and feelings adequately.

The strategies in this chapter, then, broaden the options for teachers to choose when planning reflection sessions. These alternate strategies can serve either as (1) a substitute for whole-group reflection or (2) ways of leading up to it.

The Importance of Verbalizing Thoughts and Feelings

Whatever the reflection strategy, teachers should remember the importance of having students publicly verbalize their responses to experiences. Although students can usually reflect upon experiences alone, during or shortly after having them, expressing their thoughts and feelings to the whole group provides benefits that solitary reflection cannot. Learners, for instance, model ways of sharing information with each other.

For example, if someone uses a striking metaphor to describe the feeling of seeing a large woodpecker fly close by, I might be able, for the first time, to characterize my own, similar—but unexplored—reaction to the experience. If someone, after struggling with building a fire, suddenly gains some insight about how to increase the flow of oxygen to the flame, I can discover it best if that person describes the insight for the group. Thinking out loud, whether during or after an experience, is an accepted technique for clarifying one's own reactions to the experience, as well as for helping others in the group to learn.

If I am a team member in a group assigned to build a fire, I can feel a sense of accomplishment even if I don't light the fire, so long as I have helped in the process. When I feel unprepared to do a particular task alone, but can succeed as part of a team, the group support is called "scaffolding." Perhaps I can make helpful suggestions or gather the wood, thereby contributing to the success of the project. The cooperative group enables me to share in the project, even if I lack the confidence or skills to do it alone. In the future, I am more likely to succeed in building a fire, because I was part of a successful team and because I reflected on the experience.

Another advantage of the social setting is that the excitement of my peers can motivate me to stick with the activity, even though I would be reluctant to continue it alone. For example, if I am afraid of what lives underwater, but I observe my friends enjoying themselves as they discover aquatic animals, I might change my attitude and eventually have fun doing it.

Finally, the social setting can give me a sense of importance and social status if I succeed in climbing a fourteen-foot wall or accomplish some other group challenge. With supportive norms, the social setting can enhance my sense of satisfaction, for example, when I am acknowledged for my role in achieving success during the reflection session.

These sorts of experiences, in fact, help build caring communities. That is, reflection itself becomes an experience for the community of learners. Think about it. Caine and Caine (1991, p. 87) summarize these points with this challenge: "One of our fundamental tasks as educators, therefore, is to better appreciate the social construction of knowledge."

Alternative Activities

This section presents 20 alternative activities to use in place of, or in conjunction with, structured reflection sessions based on dialogue and questioning. With a variety of strategies to serve differing needs, students are more likely to remain engaged than if they encountered the same strategy all of the time. None of us, after all, should want to teach students to dislike reflection; students who "learn" that lesson will ultimately learn little else. Teachers will be the best judges of how to select an appropriate alternative strategy and when to abandon it, if it is not helping to meet the objectives.

(1) **Metaphor making.** A metaphor is a word or phrase that is used in the place of another object, event, or idea to suggest a likeness between them. Teachers or group leaders can challenge students to create metaphors (words or phrases) that best describe a particular experience they just had.

Caine and Caine (1991, p. 115) notes that "metaphors bring with them preestablished sets of memories in which new knowledge can be embedded." Metaphor making and sharing is a way to capsulize and condense an experience and tell others what it meant in a new way. For example, a bird walk could be viewed as a colored feather hunt, or a cemetery study could be a collection of stone history books in a fenced library.

(2) **Role taking.** Students can assume different roles during the reflection session and look back on the experience through different eyes. For example, the students can describe what happened through the imagined perception of one of their classmates or even the teacher. They can even take the role of different animals, plants or aliens from another planet. They can assume the roles of the principal, guidance counselor, bank president, their mother or father, or any other community member. The point of this exercise is to help students view the experience from a new perspective, in the expectation that new meanings will emerge.

(3) **Journal entries.** Journal writing can be incorporated as a long-term project or used just once after an experience (a single entry). You can advise students that you will give them the chance to share parts of their written responses. Students, however, should have the option of declining your invitation. If the climate is supportive, most students are willing to share some or all of what they have written. Some students are even insulted if they are not able to share. Journal entries can be structured or unstructured. Some ways to structure them are to provide sentence stems which the students complete: "One question I have now is...," or "The strongest feeling during the activity was...," or "The most important learning that I gained was...."

Students can also respond to specific questions from the teacher. Preparing written responses gives some students the support and confidence they need in order to speak up in a group. Moreover, journal entries don't always have to be shared directly, but can lay the foundation for a more productive group discussion afterward.

(4) **Peer leadership.** Before conducting the outdoor experience, ask for volunteers from among the students to observe the activity and then lead the reflection session. You can structure their observations (e.g., "Look for examples of who in the group leads and who follows," or "Look for ways in which the group members work well as a team and ways in which they don't."). Alternatively, you can ask student leaders merely to identify the

key issues and topics to reflect upon afterward. Provide volunteers with some planning time to organize their reflection strategy before asking them to lead the session. You might also ask the whole group to provide constructive feedback to the leaders when the reflection session is over.

(5) **Fishbowling.** After the outdoor experience, the group can be divided in half; one half can take a seat within a circle made by the others. The outer circle forms the "fish bowl" and the inner group are the "fish." The inner group can begin by discussing the recently completed experience, either guided or unguided by the teacher. The members of the outer circle of students are not allowed to speak, but must observe the group interaction inside the circle. After a while, the outer group is asked to give their interpretation of what happened and what was said. This type of interchange can provide both halves with new insights, which they may not have discovered if they had remained in a single group after the experience.

(6) **Quote responses.** After the outdoor experience, the teacher can read some quotes to the group and ask them to relate them to what happened during the activity. This alternative, of course, requires advance preparation; but teachers can be on the lookout for useful quotes for this purpose. One can build an impressive collection after only a short time. Some of my favorites follow:

There are no passengers on spaceship earth. Everybody's crew.
> —Marshall McLuhan, quoted in
> *The Aquarian Conspiracy*

Unless someone like you cares a whole awful lot, nothing is going to get better. It's not.
> —Theodore ("Dr. Suess") Geisel, *The Lorax*

What matters is that you are not cruel or wasteful; that you don't keep the truth from those who need it, suppress someone's will or talent, take more than you need from nature, or fail to use your own talent and will.
> — Gloria Steinem, *Outrageous Acts and*
> *Everyday Rebellions*

If you are looking for a hero, look again; you are diminishing some part of yourself.
> —Sheldon Kopp, *If You Meet the*
> *Buddha on the Road, Kill Him*

Of all the teachings we receive, this one is the most important:
Nothing belongs to you of what there is,
Of what you take, you must share.
— Chief Dan George, *My Heart Soars*

You can't be ugly except to those who don't understand.
— Margery Williams, *The Velveteen Rabbit*

Argue for your limitations, and sure enough, they're yours.
—Richard Bach, *Illusions*

Convictions are potent only when they are shared. Until then, they are merely a form of daydreaming.
— Norman Cousins, *Human Options*

If you talk to animals they will talk with you
and you will know each other.
If you do not talk to them
you will not know them,
and what you do not know you will fear.
What one fears one destroys.
— Chief Dan George, *My Heart Soars*

Change our thought, and the world around us changes.
— Richard Bach, *The Bridge Across Forever*

A person cannot not communicate.
— Robert Bolton, *People Skills*

(7) **Thinking aloud.** At an appropriate point partway through an activity, the teacher can stop the group and ask someone to think aloud about the ongoing activity. The activity then continues until the teacher stops the action again. This alternative actually injects a formal reflection session into the experience as it unfolds. Thinking aloud is a good technique for helping the speaker become aware of inner talk and for others in the group to learn about how students are responding to the same situation. This is especially useful to reveal various thinking skills applied to the solution of a problem.

(8) **Positive/negative.** In order to gain two different perspectives on an activity, the teacher stops the group and asks someone to describe the activity from a positive point of view. Then after the activity continues for several minutes, the teacher stops the group and asks someone else to describe what happened from a

negative perspective. The teacher then allows the group to continue, periodically stopping them and asking for positive and negative comments about how the group is functioning. The positive and negative alternation can bring out aspects of the group that would otherwise have remained hidden. Aspects to evaluate can include: participation levels, decisionmaking, completion of tasks, group climate, cooperation, attention to guidelines, or group norms.

(9) **Imaginary videotaping.** The teacher or a committee of students assumes the role of a video camera operator and pretends to videotape part of the action. At an appropriate point, the teacher stops the action or waits for the activity to end and asks for a description of the imaginary tape. This description can include actual word-for-word comments made by some students. After the videotape description, the group discusses the accuracy of the "taped" analysis. Of course, you can also produce a real videotape (see #19, below).

(10) **Fitting the caption to the picture.** Before the activity, the teacher prepares a deck of 5 X 8 cards, each with a word or phrase describing a possible role students could play in the group. Drawing cards, one by one, students try to fit the captions written

A reflection session makes the most out of experience. (Photograph by George Tarbay, Art-Photo Dept., Northern Illinois University)

on the cards to the different roles played by students and then discuss what follows. Some possible words or phrases follow:

Words	Phrases
clown	high risk-taker
helper	low risk-taker
clarifier	someone who doesn't listen
blocker	a person who keeps score
questioner	a good coach
leader	someone who makes sure we play
observer	by the rules
dominator	person who keeps distant from the
socializer	group
	someone who follows the crowd
	someone who easily gives
	compliments

(11) **Finding feelings.** Using a list of feeling words (or writing them on separate 3 X 5 cards), ask the students to select one or two words that best describe how they feel after completing the activity. When the students have had an opportunity to express their feelings, the group can discuss their responses to probe further for possible reasons for the feelings, or for examples of behaviors or comments that may have prompted the behaviors. Such feelings might include the following:

angry	isolated
annoyed	jumpy
anxious	kind
bitter	left out
brave	mad
calm	nice
confused	nutty
defeated	overwhelmed
delighted	peaceful
disturbed	pleased
eager	refreshed
excited	sad
fearful	stunned
foolish	talkative
glad	tense
happy	uneasy
hurt	wonderful

Using books to learn more about what lives in a pond. (Photograph by Tom Lesser, Port Murray, NJ)

(12) **Diagraming and drawing.** After an activity, ask the students to diagram or draw a picture that best represents their perceptions of the way the group interacted or what the activity means to them in visual terms. In turn, each visual representation is shared with the group, if desired, and discussed.

(13) **Explaining to the principal.** The teacher tells the group that the principal is coming and wants an explanation about the last activity and the reasons why it was a valuable use of time. The

teacher or another student can role play the principal and ask the group questions that probe the importance of the activity.

(14) **Native American medicine wheel.** Locate a diagram of the Native American medicine wheel and use it to help students clarify their insights gained from an experience. In brief form, the four directions around the wheel represent different aspects of character: North = wisdom, experience, balance, and power; East = illumination and the ability to see far and wide; South = trust and innocence, seeing only what is up close; West = introspection and indecision, fear and dreaming. If a medicine wheel is marked on the ground with stones, students can physically go to each place after an activity and explain why they chose that spot. Caution: Learn as much as you can about this ritual so that you will not misrepresent it to students.

(15) **Solo experiences.** Allowing the students time alone outdoors can help them begin the process of reflection. In most cases, you should prepare students for the solo, especially if they are not accustomed to being alone outdoors. Provide them with guidelines and suggestions for getting the most out of the experience (see Appendix H for sample solo experience guidelines). After a reasonable length of time (depending upon the readiness and energy level of the students, the weather conditions, and other variables), gather the group to reflect upon the experience (see Appendix I for suggested questions for such a reflection session).

(16) **Guided field trip exercise.** After an outdoor activity, the teacher can gather the group and verbally take them through a guided field trip that has a relationship to the recently completed event. After the students listen to a three- to five-minute description, the teacher can ask them to make connections between the story and the actual event. The story could purposely take a different perspective on the completed activity and show different behaviors and attitudes of the students. The point of the exercise is to provide a point of reference with which the students can compare and contrast the actual and imagined experiences.

(17) **Silent skits.** After the outdoor experience, you can divide the group into sub-groups of three to five individuals and ask the sub-groups to prepare a silent skit (no talking allowed!). The sub-groups can choose to show how they think the group behaved or how they wished they would have behaved. After the skits, allow time for discussion of the issues raised.

(18) **Group poems, stories, and songs.** After an experience, divide the group into subgroups and ask them to write a short poem, story, or song describing the recently completed activity. Then have each small group share their creation with everyone. You can introduce different poetry forms such as limericks, haikus, cinquains, or couplets.

(19) **Videotaping or "instant" photographs.** Assign a student as the videographer or photographer to record the outdoor activity on tape or film. Then play the video or analyze an "instant" photograph as ways to recapture the event and begin the discussion.

(20) **Devil's walking stick.** This alternative concerns the idea of playing "the devil's advocate." Locate a stick to represent "the devil's walking stick." When students hold this stick, they play the devil's advocate—that is, they take positions that don't necessarily represent their own viewpoints on the topic or issue. For example, holding the stick, a student could say, "I think we worked well together," (especially if that observation were false). The stick is then passed to others, who also contribute comments they really don't believe to be true. This technique sometimes reveals perspectives that are useful for the group to know, but which might not otherwise receive adequate attention from the group.

Summary

The question-and-answer type of reflection session is the predominant model, and its aim is the cultivation of thoughtful dialogue. Alternative activities to structure reflection, however, provide variety and focus for the usual format. These activities can serve as replacements for the question-answer model or as lead-up preparation for the whole group arrangement.

Initially, the teacher is the judge in selecting and implementing the best activity structures. Ultimately, however, the students will be the final decisionmakers about which activities are most effective in bringing meaning to outdoor experiences and transferring this knowledge into action in their lives.

CHAPTER V:

Reflecting Upon the Contents of This Guidebook

Let's assume that you have read all of the chapters to this point. Even if you only read some of them, however, you can reflect upon the contents of those chapters. This chapter presents questions to help guide your reflection, and so, I have designed them to be as much about *you* as about the ideas considered in the guidebook. This is NOT a test!

Read the chapter-by-chapter questions that follow, and think about what you learned and about your teaching. Better, find some friends and tell them about your discoveries, concerns, wonderings, and other responses. Better yet, have several people read these pages or join a workshop or course on reflection and discuss your answers in a group. (See Appendix C for a checklist of possible benefits that could result from a reflection workshop.)

However you choose to ponder the meanings of your reading experience, I hope you enjoy learning more. Yes, Virginia, there is a way to learn and still have fun. Enjoy the journey!

Chapter I: Experience and Reflection—The Two Halves of Learning

(1) How do you use instructional settings outside the classroom to enrich and expand student learning? If you don't, why not?

(2) Are you aware of how reflection is used in everyday life? If so, give some examples.

(3) Do you agree that educators have been slow to incorporate reflection strategies into the schools? Explain.

(4) Which principles of "brain-based learning" had you already believed to be true, even without the research support? Which of these have you translated into teaching behavior? How?

(5) Do any of the outdoor scenarios remind you of your own teaching experiences? Which ones?

(6) Did any of the scenarios seem a little farfetched or unbelievable to you? Why might that be?

(7) Does it really matter what we call the phase in the experiential learning sequence that focuses on expanding meaning and applying it to future experience? Why or why not?

(8) Which of the many synonyms for the word "reflection" do you prefer? Why?

(9) Which definition of the reflection process do you like best? Why?

(10) Did the explanations of knowledge and knowing, thinking, experience, learning, and transfer shed any new light on the topics for you? When we use these terms without defining them, do we create communication problems sometimes?

(11) If the idea of reflection is really that old, to what extent does it (or doesn't it) fit with modern-day educational reform goals?

(12) Do most people really understand what Dewey and others meant by "learn by doing?" Can you explain the phrase using some of the new terms you have learned?

(13) After reading the first chapter, were you convinced that teachers should be using the reflection phase of learning and teaching more? What are the pluses and minuses?

Chapter II: How To Lead A Reflection Session

(14) Without a backlog of extensive research on how to lead reflection sessions, should we avoid the whole thing until we know more? Explain.

(15) Which of the six factors contributing to effective debriefing creates the biggest problem for you? Which seem the easiest to do? Explain.

(16) Which of the six factors present the biggest barriers to successfully conducting a staff development workshop in reflection for teachers? How would you suggest that the barriers be overcome?

(17) How would you characterize yourself as a teacher? (1) more comfortable when prepared with specific lesson plans or (2) more comfortable when prepared with general lesson ideas and the freedom to implement your ideas spontaneously. What implications does your answer have for conducting a reflecting session?

(18) Do you spend much time in attempting to establish a community climate that supports reflection? Why or why not? After reading about the importance of this type of climate in reflecting, do you plan any changes?

(19) Would you add any more tips for leading a reflection session to the list of 21 based on your reading or past experience? If so, what would you add? Would you cross any of the 21 items off the list? Why or why not?

Chapter III: Developing the Art and Science of Questioning

(20) Do you think that Socrates could have written the section on Socratic questioning? Explain.

(21) Which of the three forms of Socratic questioning best suits your teaching style and philosophy? Which one least suits you? Explain.

(22) Which of the different ways of categorizing questions appears to be most helpful to you in planning for reflection? Explain.

(23) Which tips for better questioning are most useful? Least useful? Explain. Would you add any tips to the list?

Chapter IV: Alternative Activities for Reflecting

(24) Even though the teacher-directed questioning approach with the whole group is the most frequently used strategy for conducting reflection, can you picture yourself using any of the alternative activities? Which ones?

(25) Does the phrase, "variety is the spice of life" apply to conducting reflection sessions? How?

Chapter V: Reflecting Upon the Contents of This Guidebook

(26) Which parts of this monograph seem to be begging you to re-read them? What might the attraction be?

(27) What is your first step in adding what you find to be the most important idea presented in the guidebook to your teaching routines?

(28) How might you enrich your curriculum by conducting a lesson outdoors? In what ways will you plan for reflecting upon that experience with your students?

(29) What additional information, structure, and support is still needed before you do more reflecting with your students? How can you get what is needed?

For information about staff development workshops in reflecting on outdoor experience, contact the author at: Box 313, Oregon IL 61061; (815) 732-3790 (home).

References

Beyer, B. K. (1987). *Practical strategies for the teaching of thinking.* Boston, MA: Allyn and Bacon, Inc.

Bitting, P. F., & Clift, R. T. (1988). Reflection upon reflection: The classical and modern views. In H. C. Waxman, H. J. Freiberg, J. C. Vaughan, & M. Well (Eds.), *Images of reflection in teacher education* (pp. 11-12). Reston, VA: Association of Teacher Education.

Boud, D., Keogh, R., & Walker, D. (Eds.). (1985). *Reflection: Turning experience into learning.* New York: Nichols Publishing Company.

Bracey, G. W. (1992). Out of context, out of mind. *Phi Delta Kappan, 73*(9), 728-729.

Brown, A. L., & Palincsar, A. S. (1989). Guided cooperative learning and individual knowledge acquisition. In L. B. Resnick (Ed.), *Knowing, learning, and instruction* (pp. 394-417). Hillsdale, NJ: Lawrence Erlbaum Associates.

Caine, R. N., & Caine, G. (1991). *Making connections: Teaching and the human brain.* Alexandria, VA: Association for Supervision and Curriculum Development.

Csikszentmihalyi, M. (1990). *Flow: The psychology of optimal experience.* New York: Harper & Row.

Dantonio, M. (1990). *How can we create thinkers? Questioning strategies that work for teachers.* Bloomington, IN: National Educational Service.

Dewey, J. (1916). *Democracy and education: An introduction to the philosophy of education.* New York: The MacMillan Company.

Duley, J. S. (1981). Field experience education. In A. W. Chickering (Ed.), *The modern American college* (pp. 600-613). San Francisco: Jossey-Bass.

Egan, G. (1973). *Face to face.* Belmont, CA: Wadsworth Publishing Company, Inc.

Fellows, K., & Zimpher, N. L. (1988). Reflectivity and the instructional process: A definitional comparison between theory and practice. In H. C. Waxman, H. J. Freiberg, J. C. Vaughan, & M. Weil (Eds.), *Images of reflection in teacher education* (pp. 18-19). Reston, VA: Association of Teacher Educators.

Frost, S. E. (1942). *Basic teachings of the great philosophers.* New York: Barnes & Noble, Inc.

Gardner, H. (1985). *Frames of mind: The theory of multiple intelligences.* New York: Basic Books.

Gass, M. (1990). Transfer of learning in adventure education. In J. C. Miles & S. Priest (Eds.), *Adventure education: A book of readings* (pp. 199-208). State College, PA: Venture Publishing, Inc.

Gaw, B. A. (1979). Processing questions: An aid to completing the learning cycle. In J. W. Pfeiffer & T. E. Jones (Eds.), *The 1979 annual handbook for group facilitators* (pp. 147-153). La Jolla, CA: University Associates, Inc.

Glasser, W. (1992). The quality school curriculum. *Phi Delta Kappan, 73*(9), 690-694.

Glenn, H. S., & Nelson, J. (1989). *Raising self-reliant children in a self-indulgent world: Seven building blocks for developing capable young people.* Rocklin, CA: Prima Publishing & Communications.

Houston, W. R. (1988). Reflecting on reflection. In H. C. Waxman, H. J. Freiberg, J. C. Vaughan, & M. Weil (Eds.), *Images of reflection in teacher education* (pp. 7-8). Reston, VA: Association of Teacher Education.

Howard, E., Howell, B. & Brainard, E. (Eds.). (1987). *Handbook for conducting school climate improvement projects.* Bloomington, IN: Phi Delta Kappa Educational Foundation.

Hunt, J., & Hitchin, P. (1989). *Creative reviewing* (2nd ed.). Cumbria, England: Groundwork Group Development.

Jones, B. F., Palincsar, A. S., Ogle, D. S., & Carr, E. G. (1987). *Strategic teaching and learning: Cognitive instruction in the content areas.* Alexandria, VA: Association for Supervision and Curriculum Development.

Jones, J. E., & Pfeiffer, J. W. (1979). Role playing. In J. E. Jones & J. W. Pfeiffer (Eds.), *The 1979 annual handbook for group facilitators* (pp. 182-193). La Jolla, CA: University Associates, Inc.

Joplin, L. (1981). On defining experiential education. *The Journal of Experiential Education, 4*(1), 17-20.

Kahn, R. (1978). The U Mass attempt to show that progressive change is still possible. *Phi Delta Kappan, 60*(2), 144-145.

Kemmis, S. (1985). Action research and the politics of reflection. In D. Boud, R. Keogh, & D. Walker (Eds.), *Reflection: Turning experience into learning* (pp. 139-163). New York: Nichols Publishing Company.

Knapp, C. E. (1984). Designing processing questions to meet specific objectives. *The Journal of Experiential Education, 7*(2), 47-49.

Knapp, C. E. (1988). *Creating humane climates outdoors: a people skills primer.* Charleston, WV: ERIC Clearinghouse on Rural Education and Small Schools.

Knapp, C. E. (1990). Processing the adventure experience. In J. C. Miles & S. Priest (Eds.), *Adventure education: A book of readings* (pp. 189-197). State College, PA: Venture Publishing, Inc.

Krathwohl, D. R., Bloom, B. S. & Masia, B. B. (1956). *Taxonomy of educational objectives* (The Classification of Educational Goals, Handbook II: Affective Domain). New York: David McKay Company, Inc.

Main, A. (1985). Reflection and the development of learning skills. In D. Boud, R. Keogh, & D. Walker (Eds.), *Reflection: Turning experience into learning* (pp. 91-99). New York: Nichols Publishing.

Marzano, R. J., Brandt, R. S., Hughes, C. S., Jones, B. F., Presseisen, B. Z., Rakin, S. C., & Suhor, C. (1988). *Dimensions of thinking.* Alexandria, VA: The Association for Supervision and Curriculum Development.

Meyers, C. (1987). *Teaching students to think critically.* San Francisco: Jossey-Bass Publishers.

Palmer, A. B. (1981). Learning cycles: Models of behavioral change. In J. W. Pfeiffer & J. E. Jones (Eds.), *The 1981 annual handbook for group facilitators* (pp. 147-154). San Diego, CA: University Associates, Inc.

Paul, R., & Binker, A. J. A. (1990). Socratic questioning. In R. Paul (Ed.), *Critical Thinking* (pp. 269-298). Rohnert Park, CA: Center for Critical Thinking and Moral Critique.

Pearson, M., & Smith, D. (1988). Debriefing in experience-based learning. In D. Boud, et al. (Eds.). *Reflection: turning experience into learning* (pp. 69-84). New York: Nichols Publishing Company.

Perkins, D. N., & Salomon, G. (1988). Teaching for transfer. *Educational Leadership, 46*(1), 22-32.

Pinar, W. F., & Grumet, M. P. (1976). *Toward a poor curriculum.* Dubuque, IA: Kendall/Hunt Publishing.

Pugach, M. C., & Johnson, L. J. (1988). Promoting teacher reflection through structured dialogue. In H. C. Waxman, H. J. Freiberg, J. C. Vaughan, & M. Weil (Eds.), *Images of reflection in teacher education* (pp. 30-31). Reston, VA: Association of Teacher Educators.

Quinsland, L. K., & Van Ginkel, A. (1984). How to process experience. *The Journal of Experiential Education, 7*(2), 8-13.

Resnick, L. B. (1987). *Education and learning to think.* Washington, D.C., National Academy Press.

Resnick, L. B. (Ed.). (1989). *Knowing, learning, and instruction.* Hillsdale, NJ: Lawrence Erlbaum Associates.

Resnick, L. B., & Klopfer, L. E. (Eds.). (1989). *Toward the thinking curriculum: Current cognitive research.* Alexandria, VA: Association for Supervision and Curriculum Development.

Rowe, M. B. (1987). Using wait time to stimulate inquiry. In W. W. Wilen (Ed.), *Questioning, questioning techniques, and effective teaching.* Washington, DC: National Education Association.

Sarason, S. B. (1984). [Review of *Schooling in America: Scapegoat and salvation* by Vernon H. Smith]. *Phi Delta Kappan, 66*(3), pp. 224-225.

Schön, D. A. (1983). *The reflective practitioner: How professionals think in action.* New York: Basic Books, Inc.

Staff. (1991, December). Raise math and science achievement, panel urges. *ASCD Update,* p. 6.

Staff. (Spring/Summer, 1990). The Foxfire approach: Perspectives and core practices. *Hands On, A Journal For Teachers* (The Foxfire Fund, Inc.)

Vygotsky, L. S. (1978). *Mind in society.* Cambridge, MA: Harvard University Press.

Walter, G. A. & Marks, S. E. (1981). *Experiential learning and change.* New York: John Wiley and Sons.

Wertheimer, M. (1945). *Productive thinking.* New York: Harper and Row.

Whitehead, A. N. (1929). *The aims of education and other essays.* New York: The New American Library.

Wigginton, E. (1986). *Sometimes a shining moment: The Foxfire experience.* New York: Doubleday.

Appendices

Key Questions about Reflecting on Outdoor Activities

1. What can people learn about themselves and others by participating in outdoor activities?

2. What is your view of how people learn from experience?

3. What is your view of human nature, in general, and the group members you are teaching, in particular?

4. What norms and ground rules will promote personal growth (intrapersonal skills) and community building (interpersonal skills)?

5. What objectives are appropriate for guiding the reflection session? (How would you like the participants to change?)

6. What criteria are useful in selecting specific outdoor activities?

7. Does the group understand the role of outdoor activities in reaching specific objectives?

8. Can you identify some key issues (e.g., sex-role stereotyping, lack of trust, poor communication, ineffective decisionmaking) operating in the group? How will you decide on which issues to reflect upon?

9. How flexible are you in adapting the design plan as the group develops?

10. How does your preferred leadership style and personality type affect your ability to lead a reflection session?

11. How do the different leadership styles and personality types in the group affect the interpersonal dynamics?

12. When is it appropriate to participate in the outdoor activity with the group?

13. At what point should you share the chosen objectives with the group?

14. How do you know if the group dynamics are getting too complex for your level of expertise?

15. What skills are needed to reflect upon group experience? How can you develop more of these skills in order to improve your teaching?

16. What is a logical sequence to follow for asking questions and sharing observations?

17. What is the proper balance between divergent and convergent questions?

18. What is the non-verbal language in the group communicating?

19. When is it appropriate for you to paraphrase participant responses?

20. How much and often should you give short lectures about your observations of group development or human relations?

21. How much participant-to-participant dialogue occurs? How can such interaction be increased?

22. How much "wait time" do you provide after asking questions (wait-time-1) and after students respond (wait-time-2)?

23. How much time should be spent reflecting compared to doing the outdoor activities? Should every activity be reflected upon?

24. How do you respond emotionally to certain behaviors and feelings in the group, for example, conflict, anger, fear, sadness, joy?

Preparing To Lead A Group:
Questions To Ask Yourself

The following questions are designed to help you become clearer about some issues of group leadership.

1. What is the main purpose of the group experience?

2. Specifically, what do you expect to accomplish in the time allotted?

3. How will you go about reaching these objectives?

4. How would you describe your primary leadership style?

5. What are your strengths and which areas need improvement for you to become a more effective group leader?

6. How can you use your strengths most productively?

7. Can you predict some potential problems (based on what you know about the group and yourself?)

8. How do you feel today? Is anything happening in your life that may interfere with your ability to give full attention to the needs of the group?

9. Are you looking forward to beginning this group session? Why or why not?

10. What do you most want to happen in the group today?

11. How do you plan to begin the group?

12. How much structure will you provide and to what extent will you allow the group to create its own structure?

13. What specific norms or ground rules would you like to establish in the group? How will you influence the formation of such norms or ground rules?

14. To what extent will you participate as a group member, and to what extent will you stay in the "leader" role?

15. What plans have you made to achieve closure and to summarize and evaluate the accomplishments of your group?

Checklist of Possible Benefits From a Reflection Workshop

_____ 1. To get to know the group better and develop a better sense of community.

_____ 2. To practice certain interpersonal and intrapersonal skills useful for understanding group dynamics.

_____ 3. To become more aware of group norms and expected "ground rules" that promote a sense of community.

_____ 4. To clarify several key goals and objectives for reflection sessions following experiences.

_____ 5. To develop sets of pre-planned reflection questions to achieve selected objectives.

_____ 6. To develop a list of sequential steps and tips for conducting a reflection session.

_____ 7. To clarify a code of ethics for conducting reflection sessions.

_____ 8. To identify key group process issues that could be reflected upon.

_____ 9. To develop criteria for selecting key issues and topics to reflect upon.

_____ 10. To clarify a personal philosophy about how people learn through group experiences.

____ 11. To develop a list of dos and don'ts to remember while in the role of group facilitator.

____ 12. To develop guidelines for designing a reflection session and to develop criteria for deciding when to deviate from that plan.

____ 13. To clarify the reasons that individuals may have for participating in outdoor experiences.

____ 14. To analyze your personal behaviors in a group as a means of better understanding group process.

____ 15. To identify a personal change or changes to be made and to develop a plan to implement these changes in your life.

Checking For A Sense of Community

(from Knapp, 1988, pp. 3-4)

People generally experience a sense of community when they become aware of certain positive factors operating in a group. What do you, personally, consider to be some indicators of a sense of community? What elements do you believe need to be present among the participants in a caring community?

Directions:

In column 1, rate each item according to how much you agree that factor is necessary for a sense of community.

In column 2, rate each item according to whether you now experience that factor in your group.

In column 3, rate each item according to how much you would like to experience that factor in your group.

Using ratings from 0-10 (10 is the highest), rate the following items.

"I feel a sense of community when I. . .   1   2   3

. . .empathize with other's thoughts and
    feelings.   ___ ___ ___

. . .want to include others and be included
    in a group.   ___ ___ ___

	1	2	3
. . .build others up in person and in their absence.	—	—	—
. . .show helpful support when it is needed.	—	—	—
. . .feel that I need people to support my ideals.	—	—	—
. . .feel strong emotion on issues that relate to others in the group.	—	—	—
. . .allow myself to trust and become vulnerable to a certain extent.	—	—	—
. . .demonstrate that I care about maintaining the relationships of the group.	—	—	—
. . .am appropriately self-disclosing and honest in my communication.	—	—	—
. . .want to know about and seek out information about the others in the group.	—	—	—
. . .want to join with others to complete agreed upon tasks cooperatively.	—	—	—
. . .believe I have a sense of power and control in deciding the direction the group can take.	—	—	—

APPENDIX E

Reflection Questions

After completing the three columns of the exercise presented in Appendix D, ask yourself the following questions:

1. Are certain community indicators more important to you in certain groups?

2. Can you add any community indicators that you believe are essential in some groups?

3. Are there any community indicators that you believe don't belong in the list?

4. Were some community indicators difficult for you to rate? Why was this so?

5. Which community indicators did you rate below where you would have liked them to be? What can you do about this situation?

6. What are some ways in which you block yourself from rating certain indicators higher? What are some ways in which others block you from rating them higher?

7. Can you make an action plan that would help you feel more of a sense of community in the group you selected? If so, do it!

What Have You Learned and How Did You Learn It?

A Way to Reflect Upon an Outdoor Experience

1. What do you know now that you didn't know before? (Knowing something, in this case, means mentally recalling and communicating it by verbalizing, demonstrating it in other ways upon request, or justifying its importance and use.)

2. What attitudes and feelings do you have about the experience that you didn't have before? (Attitudes are personal preferences or dislikes and feelings are emotional states such as being mad, scared, sad, or glad.)

3. Are you aware of any other changes that occurred in knowledge, skills, attitudes, or feelings as a direct result of this experience? If so, explain.

4. What do you think you will remember or retain in other ways after the experience? Can you explain why this might be so?

5. What will you probably verbally share with or demonstrate to others in the future?

6. How did you actually learn what is most important to you?

    a. Heard it told by the teacher.

    b. Heard it told by one of your peers.

    c. Observed or discovered it myself without outside help.

    d. Became aware of it through a small or large group discussion.

    e. Other ways? What are they?

Evaluating Yourself and The Group

1. What activities or exercises were most valuable for you? Why?

2. How has this group met your needs?

3. How have you contributed to the group? (Contributions relate to personal qualities you possess and roles you've played.)

4. Would you make any personal changes in how you will contribute to groups in the future?

5. What are some things that would have made the group experience better for you?

6. What are some things you appreciate about the members of this group?

7. What changes would you suggest for future group experiences?

8. Where does this group go from here?

9. Other comments about yourself and the group.

Solo Experience Guidelines and Reflection Questions

A solo experience is an opportunity to reflect on your life by yourself in a natural setting. Usually, a person does not move from the assigned spot and doesn't communicate with people until later. You may want to record your impressions on paper or just think about them.

One approach is to focus on the present and make connections with the environment. You may:

- Watch plants grow and move.

- Observe animals.

- Use as many senses as possible to examine something.

- Explore the soil.

- Do other things, but always "staying in the present."

Another approach is to focus on the recent past. Think about:

- What have the past few days meant to you as a student, as a family member, as a member of a peer group, and so forth?

- What experiences have changed you and how?

- What have you most enjoyed or benefitted from?

- What was most difficult or challenging?

Another approach is to focus on the future. Consider the following:

- What would you do differently if you were starting this solo again tomorrow?

- How might you change your life when you return to the regular routine?

- How might this experience affect your personal life?

- Other goals or plans...for next year...for five years...for 10 years from now.

A fourth approach is to balance your thoughts and feelings about the present, past, and future or to clear your mind of thoughts and feelings and just "be." Some ideas to think about:

- How does nature affect you?

- Are there lessons to be learned from nature that relate to how you interact with people?

- Is nature really separate from people?

- Is it possible to be alone and not be lonely?

- What are your personal strengths that will help you succeed in life?

Enjoy your solo experience by making the most of your time alone. Be prepared to share verbally some of your insights with others afterwards.

Reflecting Upon the Solo Experience

Directions: After the students complete the solo, bring them together to think about and discuss the following questions:

1. Which of the four approaches to the solo did you choose? Why?

2. What were some important things that happened to you during your time alone?

3. Did anything happen to cause you to feel uncomfortable in any way? If so, explain.

4. Did you mainly focus on the environment around you or the environment within yourself? Is that typical of you?

5. Did you do more thinking than feeling or more feeling than thinking? In general, would you describe yourself more as a thinker, feeler, or both?

6. Were you tempted to move toward someone else and start a conversation? How important is talking and being with people to you?

7. What will you remember most from this solo experience? Can you explain why you might remember these things?

8. How might this solo help you when you return to your normal routine?

9. If you were limited to one word that best represents the significance of the solo experience for you, what would that word be?

Reflecting Upon A Cooperative Experience

1. Who assumed the leadership?

2. How was this leadership shown?

3. Who assumed the followship?

4. How was this followship shown?

5. How did each group member contribute to the task?

6. Did everyone follow the rules? If not, why not?

7. What awareness of nature, human nature, or both resulted?

8. How did the activity impact the quality of the area?

9. What did you think about that you didn't say out loud?

10. How would you do this differently next time?

APPENDIX K

Guiding Children's Learning

Note: Carl Rogers[1] asked himself what he would need to find out if he were given the responsibility of guiding the learning of a group of children. He came up with a list of questions revolving around six important personal skill areas. These skills were: 1) being empathic, 2) taking risks, 3) unleashing curiosity, 4) providing physical and psychological resources, 5) encouraging creativity, and 6) nurturing feelings and intellect. Here is a partial list of some of the questions that Rogers would ask as a facilitator of learning:

1. What is it like to be a child who is learning something significant?

2. Do I dare to let myself deal with this boy or girl as a person, as someone I respect?

3. Do I dare reveal myself to him and let him reveal himself to me?

4. Do I dare to recognize that he may know more than I do in certain areas - or may in general be more gifted than I?

5. What are the things that excite them, and how can I find out?

6. How can I preserve and unleash curiosity?

7. How can I imaginatively provide resources for learning—resources that are both physically and psychologically available?

8. Do I have the tolerance and humanity to accept annoying, occasionally defiant, occasionally oddball questions of some of those who have creative ideas?

9. Can I help the students develop a feeling life as well as a cognitive life?

---

[1]Rogers, C. (1983). *Freedom to Learn For the 80's.* Columbus, OH: Charles E. Merrill Publishing Company, 137-142.

What Is Significant Learning?

Note: Rogers[2] believes that significant learning is more than an accumulation of facts. "It is a learning which makes a difference—in the individual's behavior, in the course of action he chooses in the future, in his activities and in his personality."

* The person comes to see himself differently.

* He accepts himself and his feelings more fully.

* He becomes more self-confident and self-directing.

* He becomes more the person he would like to be.

* He becomes more flexible, less rigid, in his perceptions.

* He adopts more realistic goals for himself.

* He behaves in a more mature fashion.

* He changes his maladjustive behaviors....

* He becomes more acceptant of others.

* He becomes more open to the evidence, both to what is going on outside himself, and to what is going on inside himself.

* He changes in his basic personality characteristics, in constructive ways.

I think perhaps this is sufficient to indicate that these are learnings which are significant, which do make a difference.

Creating Humane Climates

Rogers believes that..."the task of the teacher is to create a facilitating... climate in which significant learning can take place."[3]

To think and write on:

1. What questions do you ask yourself before you prepare to teach a lesson?

---

[2]Rogers, C. (1961). *On Becoming A Person.* Boston: Houghton Mifflin Company, 280-281.

[3]Ibid, 287.

2. Do you disagree with any of the questions Rogers asks himself? If so, which ones? Why?

3. What does significant learning mean to you?

4. Recall an instance of significant learning for you. What characteristics were present for that to occur?

5. Do you disagree with any of the characteristics of significant learning that Rogers describes? If so, which ones? Why?

6. Which personal skills do you currently possess that enable you to facilitate significant learning for people?

7. Which skills would you like to develop or refine that you don't possess to the degree you would like now?

Outdoor/Environmental/ Experiential Education Resources

Organizations

The American Camping Association
Bradford Woods
5000 State Road 67 North
Martinsville, IN 46151-7902

Primarily devoted to organizational camping on the national level. Periodical - *Camping Magazine*

The Association for Experiential Education
2885 Aurora Avenue #28
Boulder, CO 80303-2252
(303) 440-8844

Dedicated to the promotion of adventure-based and experiential learning programs. Periodicals - *The AEE Horizon Newsletter* and *The Journal of Experiential Education*

Foundation for Community Encouragement
109 Danbury Road
Ridgefield, CT 06877
(203) 431-9489

Devoted to the development of community building skill. Periodical - *Communiqué*

International Association for the Study of Cooperation in Education
Box 1582
Santa Cruz, CA 95061-1582
(408) 426-7926

Promotes all aspects of cooperation in education. Periodical -

Cooperative Learning (Note especially the 1990 special edition resource guide - Vo. 11, No. 1)

National Association for Mediation in Education
425 Amity Street
Amherst, MA 01002
(413) 545-2462

Devoted to promoting conflict resolution and peacemaking programs in education. Periodical - bi-monthly newsletter

National Society for Internships and Experiential Education
3509 Haworth Drive, Suite 207
Raleigh, NC 27609
(919) 787-3263

Supports the use of learning through experience as an integral part of education. Periodical - *Experiential Education Newsletter*

North American Association for Environmental Education
5995 Horseshoe Bend Road, P.O. Box 400
Troy, OH 45373
(513) 698-6493

Promotes the analysis and understanding of environmental issues and questions as the basis for effective education. Periodical - *The Environmental Communicator*

Wilderness Education Association
20 Winona Avenue, Box 89
Saranac Lake, NY 12983
(518) 891-2915

Promotes professionalization of outdoor leadership to enhance the conversation of the wild outdoors. Periodical - *WEA Legend*

Networks/Coalitions

Alliance for Environmental Education
Box 368, 51 Main Street
The Plains, VA 22171-0368
(703) 253-5812

A cooperative alliance of business, industry, and environmental organizations devoted to communication of information and viewpoints on environmental issues. Periodical - *The Alliance Exchange* and other mailings

Coalition for Education in the Outdoors
P.O. Box 2000
Park Center
Cortland, NY 13045
(607) 753-4941

A network of organizations, businesses, institutions, centers, agencies and associations linked and communicating in support of the board purposes of educating in, for and about the outdoors. Periodical - *The Taproot*

The Global Alliance for Transforming Education
4202 Ashwoody Trail
Atlanta, GA 30319
(404) 458-5678

Promotes a vision of education that fosters personal greatness, social justice, peace, and a sustainable environment. Periodical - newsletters and other information

Human Relations Skills Network for Outdoor Leaders
ACA: Illinois Section
67 East Madison Street, Suite 1406
Chicago, IL 60603-3010
(312) 332-0833

Focused on theory and practice in human relations in schools, camps, outdoor centers, and religious institutions. Periodical - *Human Relations Skills Network Newsletter*

National Consortium on Alternatives for Youth at Risk, Inc.
5250 17th Street, Suite 107
Sarasota, FL 34235
(813) 378-4793

Devoted to distributing information related to youth at risk. Periodical - "Green Sheets" on various topics

The Outdoor Network
P.O. Box 2269
Boulder, CO 80306-2269
(303) 938-6866

Devoted to information and education related to all aspects of outdoor use and programming. Periodical - *The Outdoor Network Newsletter*

Colleges and Universities

Aurora University
Recreation Administration Department
327 S. Gladstone Avenue
Aurora, IL 60506
(708) 844-5404

Contact: Dr. Rita Yerkes, Associate Dean, George Williams College

University of Wisconsin
College of Natural Resources
UW - Stevens Point
Stevens Point, WI 54481
(715) 346-2853

Contact: Dr. Richard Wilke

Indiana University
Bradford Woods Outdoor Education Center
5040 State Road 67 North
Martinsville, IN 46151
(317) 342-2915

Contact: Gary Robb

Northeastern Illinois University
Health and Physical Education Department
5500 North St. Louis Avenue
Chicago, IL 60625-4699
(312) 794-2982

Contact: Dr. William Quinn

Northern Illinois University
Lorado Taft Field Campus
Box 299
Oregon, IL 61061
(815) 732-2111

Contact: Dr. Clifford E. Knapp

Selected Books on Education, Reflection and Experiential Education

Gass, M.A. (1993). *Adventure Therapy: Therapeutic Applications of Adventure Programming.* Dubuque, IA: Kendall/Hunt Publishing Company.

Kalisch, K. R. (1979). *The role of the Instructor in Outward Bound Educational Process.* Published by the author: Honey Rock Camp, Northwoods Campus, Wheaton College, Three Lakes, WI 54562

Kraft, R. & Sakofs, M. (n.d.) *The theory of experiential education.* Boulder, CO: Association for Experiential Education.

Miles, J. C. & Priest, S. (1990). *Adventure education.* State College, PA: Venture Publishing, Inc.

Nadler, R. S. & Luckner, J. L. (1992). *Processing the adventure experience.* Dubuque, IA: Kendall/Hunt Publishing Company.

Schoel, J., Prouty, D. & Radcliffe, P. (1988). *Islands of healing.* Hamilton, MA: Project Adventure, Inc.

Smith, T.E. et al. (1992). *The Theory and Practice of Challenge Education.* Dubuque, IA: Kendall/Hunt Publishing Company.

A Bibliography for Expanding Awareness of Reflection and Personal and Interpersonal Growth

Note: Occasionally people ask about the books that have contributed to my understanding of personal growth and people skills. This bibliography contains some of these works by people who have made a difference in my life. For their ideas I am truly grateful.   — C.E.K.

Auvine, B. et al. (1978). *A manual for group facilitators.* Madison, WI: The Center for Conflict Resolution (731 State Street 53703).

Corey, and Cory, M. S. (1982). *Groups: process and practice.* (2nd Ed.). Monterey, CA: Brooks/Cole Publishing Company.

Carkuff, R. R. (1983). *The art of helping.* (5th Ed.). Amherst, MA: Human Resource Press, Inc. (22 Amherst Road 01002).

Egan, G. (1973). *Face to face.* Belmont, CA: Wadsworth Publishing Company, Inc. (94002).

Ellis, A. and Harper, R. A. (1978). *A new guide to rational living.*

North Hollywood, NA: Wilshire Book Company. (12015 Sherman Road 91605).

Fisher, R. and Ury, W. (1983). *Getting to yes: negotiating agreement without giving in.* NY: Viking Penguin Inc. (40 West 23rd Street 10010).

Gordon, T. and Burch, N. (1974). T.E.T.: *Teacher effectiveness training.* NY: Peter H. Wyden/Publisher.

Jackins, H. (1972). *The human side of human beings.* Seattle, WA: Rational Island Publishers (P.O. Box 2081, Main Office Station, 98111).

Jackins, H. (1973). *The human situation.* Seattle, WA: Rational Island Publishers. (P.O. Box 2081, Main Office Station, 98111).

Napier, R. W. and Gershenfeld, M. K. (1983). *Making groups work: A guide for group leaders.* Boston, MA: Houghton Mifflin Company.

Napier, R. W. and Gershenfeld, M. K. (1973). *Groups: theory and experience.* Boston, MA: Houghton Mifflin Company. (Accompanied by an Instructor's manual).

Peck, M. S. (1987). *The different drum.* NY: Simon and Schuster.

Rogers, C. R. (1980). *A way of being.* Boston, MA: Houghton Mifflin Company.

Rogers, C. R. (1983). *Freedom to learn for the 80's.* Columbus, OH: Charles E. Merrill Publishing Company.

Satir, V. (1972). *Peoplemaking.* Palo Alto, CA: Science and Behavior Books, Inc.

Satir, V. (1978). *Your many faces.* Millbrae, CA: Celestial Arts. (231 Ardian Road, 94030).

Annotated Bibliograpy
Cooperative Games/Challenges

Fleugelman, Andrew. (1976). *The New Games Book.* New York: Doubleday and Company. p. 194.

This is the "bible" of cooperative games. The activities are broken into the categories of "very active," "active," and "moderate." They are further sectioned for the number of participants.

Fleugelman, Andrew. (1981) *More New Games*. New York: Doubleday and Company. p. 190.

This book makes modifications on the first one (above), as well as including more great games. It has the same organizational structure, and is at least as good.

Orlik, Terry. (1971). *Winning Through Cooperation*. Washington, DC: Acropolis Books, LTD. p. 178.

Orlik is a physical educator by profession. These activities are geared towards students in such an environment. The majority of his ideas are designed for pre-kindergarten to 6th grade children.

Rohnke, Karl. (1985). *Silver Bullets*. Hamilton, MA: Project Adventure, Inc. p. 186.

Rohnke has included about 150 activities; categorized into four sections: "Games," "Trust," "Initiatives," "Stunts." Of all the books in the field, this is the most creative.

Rohnke, Karl. (1989). *Cowtails and Cobras II*. Dubuque, IA: Kendall/Hunt Publishing Co. p. 120.

The subtitle of the book is "a guide to ropes courses, initiatives games, and other adventure activities. Most of the book deals with the construction and use of a ropes course.

Sanborne, Jane. (1984). *Bag of Tricks*. Florissant, CO: Search Publications. p. 125.

Included in this book are 180 creative games of various types. There are chapters on "Initiatives," "Night Activities," "Nature Games," "Dramatics," "Cooperative Games," and more. The title describes this book quite well.

Weinstein, Matt and Goodman, Joel. (1986). *Playfair*. San Louis Obispo, CA: Impact Publishers. p. 249.

This is an excellent compilation of cooperative games for people of all ages. Chapters include topics such as: "Mixer Games," "Learning Games," "Games for Leadership Training," and "Mind Games." Included also are some suggestions for the debriefing process.

ABOUT THE AUTHOR

Dr. Knapp is a professor of outdoor teacher education at Northern Illinois University's Lorado Taft Field Campus in Oregon, Illinois. He has been a teacher and administrator in grades K-12, as well as a teacher educator during his 30-year career. His special interests are in environmental ethics and values, curriculum and instruction in outdoor and environmental education, and human relations skills and activities outdoors. He has been an author or co-author of several other ERIC/CRESS publications including: *Using the Outdoors To Teach Social Studies* (1986), *Creating Humane Climates Outdoors* (1988), and a recent ERIC Digest on the same topic as this guidebook.